THE STORY OF THE STUPA

FRONTISPIECE.

GANDHARA SCULPTURES SHOWING TWO KINDS OF CEREMONIAL UMBRELLAS (CIRCA 200 A.D.).

THE STORY OF THE STUPA

A. H. LONGHURST

GYAN

Published by

Gyan Publishing House
5, Ansari Road
Daryaganj, New Delhi-110002
Phone: 011-47034999, 9811692060
E-mail: books@gyanbooks.com

Distribution Network
gyanbooks.com
India, USA, Canada, UK, Australia, France

ISBN : 978-81-212-4069-7 (PB)
First Published, 1936

2nd Impression 2020

Printed at: Gyan Press, Delhi.

The Story of the Stupa
Author: A. H. Longhurst

The Story of the Stūpa

BY

A. H. LONGHURST,

Archæological Commissioner,

Ceylon.

(Late Supdt., Archæological Survey, India.)

Printed at the Ceylon Government Press, Colombo.

1936.

CONTENTS.

LIST OF ILLUSTRATIONS.

3---J. N. 56882 (6/36)

NOTE.

The photographs reproduced in this book are from blocks prepared by the Survey Department, Colombo.

The Story of the Stūpa.

CHAPTER I.

The Umbrella as a Symbol of Religious Sovereignty.

As a symbol of authority and power, the umbrella first appears in the mural paintings of the Ancient Egyptians, and later in the bas-reliefs of the Assyrians. Many Egyptian pictures dating hundreds of years before the bas-reliefs of the Assyrians, portray the umbrella as an appendage of a priest or prince ; whilst some of the Assyrian sculptures show slaves holding a richly ornamented umbrella above the head of the monarch, not only in scenes of peace, but even in time of war. Some good examples of these Assyrian umbrellas dating back to the eighth century B.C., may be seen among the bas-reliefs in the Nineveh Gallery of the British Museum. They appear to have been of wood covered with cloth and usually fringed with tassels. Some are conical in shape, while others have round, wheel-like canopies like those depicted in the earliest Buddhist bas-reliefs. Similar scenes are reported to be represented in some of the ancient sculptures of Persepolis. We know that the Greeks used the umbrella as a mark of elevated rank, the custom being borrowed from the earlier empires, but after the rise of the Roman power the umbrella seems to have lost its royal significance in Europe.

It is in Asia, however, that the umbrella plays such an important part in the life and history of the people. Here it is not only a symbol of sovereignty, but partakes of a religious character, and it is sometimes an object of veneration. This is particularly the case in Buddhist countries like Burma, Siam, and China.

We do not know how or when the umbrella first became the recognized symbol of authority in India, but from the singular resemblance between the umbrellas portrayed in the earliest Buddhist sculptures and those

4——J. N. 55882 (6/36)

portrayed in the still earlier Assyrian and Persian bas-reliefs, there seems good reason to assume that it was from Persia that the idea first came, which led to its adoption in India as the emblem of sovereignty.

In the earliest Buddhist sculptures, the umbrella is reserved exclusively as a mark of distinction for the monarchs or princes portrayed in the bas-reliefs, except where it appears in the service of religion, when it is used as a means of denoting the presence of the Buddha. In early Buddhist art images of the Buddha never appear; he is always represented by a religious symbol, such as a wheel, a throne, a pair of footprints, the Bodhi-tree, &c.; and as a rule, these representations of sacred symbols are shown as being overshadowed by one or more honour-conferring umbrellas.

From the earliest times down to the present day two kinds of ceremonial umbrellas have been in use in India. One has a large domed canopy and the other is of the usual wheel-like type. Both are made of wood, covered with coloured cloth or silk, ornamented with a fringe and surmounted by a brass or gilt-copper finial. They are usually very large and measure from 4 to 6 feet in diameter, and the staffs are about 8 feet high; they are carried above the heads of the Jain and Hindu images when the latter are taken in procession during the big car-festivals. The two kinds of sunshades are portrayed in the Gandhāra sculptures shown in the Frontispiece and which date back to about the third century A.D., and two modern examples from the Madras Presidency are illustrated in Figs. 1 and 2. It is clear from these early sculptures, that ceremonial umbrellas similar in every way to those still in use, were used by the Gandhāra Buddhists in the earliest days of Buddhism; and, as a symbol of sovereignty, it was no doubt common in India long before the advent of Buddhism.

Regarding the singular reverence bestowed on the umbrella as proved from the earliest Buddhist sculptures, none are more interesting than those which suggest the retention of primitive Tree-worship in the earliest days of pure Buddhism. Many of the bas-reliefs belonging to the gateways of the famous Sāñchī Stūpa in Bhopāl State portray sacred trees hung with garlands and overshadowed by single- or double-canopied umbrellas, and approached by crowds of worshippers both human and celestial.

Until the conquest of India by the British, the use of the umbrella was jealously reserved as a royal prerogative by the Muhammadan rulers. When European travellers or traders entered the city of Delhi, they invariably had to dispense with their sunshades, so as not to infringe the rights of the Great Mogul. It is interesting to note that when our present King was last touring in India a state umbrella was held above his head, as a symbol of royalty, at all official functions.

The magnificence of these Indian state umbrellas was amazing. Some were of crimson velvet richly embroidered in gold, and the heavy golden handles, which were 8 feet high, were encrusted with precious stones. That of the Queen of Lucknow, which is now treasured in the South Kensington Museum, is of blue satin embroidered with gold and seed pearls. Some were of cloth of gold, others only of gilt paper and a few were even covered with gay feathers, but all had long handles, either of inlaid wood or of gold, or even of carved ivory. The state umbrellas of Buddhist countries like China, Siam, and Burma are most gorgeous in appearance, and have a number of superimposed canopies upon one pole. The canopies are of silks of varied colours, richly embroidered with sacred or national emblems. In China, one of the main features of a coronation or royal wedding is a great procession of these state umbrellas. The number of these emblems, all carried by high officials, sometimes reaches the high figure of two hundred. According to the celebrated Chinese pilgrim Hiuen Tsang, who visited India in the seventh century A.D., similar processions took place in the Panjāb, as he tells of a grand ceremonial which he saw in Peshāwar at which "three hundred umbrellas of rich material were carried in the procession"; so in all probability, this custom was introduced into China along with the Buddhist religion from India.

In China, the umbrella which is so highly prized by the living is also esteemed an acceptable offering to the dead. Hence, in those strange cities of the dead, which exist in the neighbourhood of many Chinese cemeteries where, each in his own hired house, the coffins of the wealthy dead are detained perhaps for years, awaiting the auspicious day for burial, umbrellas, which at first glance appear to be identical with those of the mandarins, stand open beside the coffin. A closer inspection, however, proves them to be only made of paper and tinsel, as are most other objects offered to the dead in the Far East.

In all Buddhist countries, even at the present day, handsome state umbrellas hold a distinguished place in all important funeral ceremonies. In Siam, we find a unique feature in connection with the use of the umbrella at funerals. When a wealthy man or a high official departs this life, his body is embalmed and placed in a country boat which is covered in at the top and serves as a coffin. Then, in the centre of the boat, a lofty pole decorated with a number of superimposed umbrella canopies is erected, the number of canopies varying according to the rank and social importance of the deceased. The boat is launched on a river and allowed to drift whither it likes, burial or cremation taking place near the spot where the funeral boat eventually strands. Two engravings of these Siamese funeral boats are shown in Kamepfer's *History of Japan*, published in 1727. One of these boats has a tall pyramidal tower of wooden construction surmounted by a tall triple canopied umbrella. In the other the tower itself consists of ten canopies fixed upon a single lofty pole, suggesting the form of a Japanese wooden pagoda of many storeys.

In all these cases the object to be attained is honour to relics of the dead, which is precisely the original intention of the storeyed pagoda of the East. But in China in later times, however, this primary purpose seems to have been abandoned, and many of the more recent masonry-built pagodas have been erected solely with a view to geomantic influences, the tall towers being supposed to have some mysterious effect on that strange, undefinable *Fung Shui*—the mystic spirit of the mighty Dragon who rules over wind and water, and controls all human destinies. Several of the finest nine-storeyed pagodas in the neighbourhood of Canton were erected for this purpose, in the belief that by their means lurking evils would be dispelled, and the general peace and prosperity of the province insured.

The custom of erecting these temporary wooden pagodas over the dead still prevails on the West Coast of India and in Burma, and, according to Hiuen Tsang, it existed in Northern India in the days of the Buddha. In describing the funeral procession and cremation of the body of the Buddha at Kusinārā (*circa* 487 B.C.), he says that when the Buddha died, " men and *devas*, moved with love, prepared a coffin made of the seven precious substances, and in a thousand cloths swathed his body, they spread both flowers and perfumes, and placed canopies and umbrellas above (the bier). Then the host of the Mallas raised the bier and forward marched, with others following and leading on. Passing the golden river (*Kin-ho*) to the north, they filled the coffin up with scented oil, and piled high the odorous wood and kindled it."[1] After the cremation of the body, the ashes were collected and a brick *stūpa* built over them to mark the spot where the great ceremony

[1] Beal's Records of the Western World, Vol. II, p 39.

took place. The accuracy of this description, is to some extent, confirmed by the Gandhāra bas-reliefs shown in Figs. 3 and 4, which were executed several centuries before the birth of Hiuen Tsang. In Fig. 3, we have a representation of the death of the Great Teacher, who is portrayed lying on a wooden cot similar to those in use in India at the present day. Grouped round the bed are the " men and *devas* " mentioned by Hiuen Tsang. The Indo-Corinthian capitals of the pilasters flanking the panel indicate that the sculpture was executed when Greek influence in Indian art was still strong in the Peshāwar district. The next scene depicts the funeral-car surmounted by a large state umbrella with two monks in attendance (Fig. 4). Owing to the restricted height of the panel, which had to be uniform in size with the others, the artist was unable to portray a lofty pole supporting a number of superimposed canopies as described by the Chinese pilgrim. However, crudely executed as the sculpture is, it is quite clear that the domed canopy below and the big umbrella above it are represented as being fixed one above the other on the same staff in the usual manner of the present day. The last scene shows two Mallas holding oil-ladles superintending the cremation of the body.

This ancient funeral custom still survives amongst the Buddhist monks of Burma. Immediately after death, the body of a Burmese monk is embalmed, a sarcophagus is prepared for it, painted with scenes from the life of the Buddha. A special temporary wooden building or shrine is then erected, where the body lies in state. When the time for the cremation ceremony arrives, a many-canopied wooden funeral-car, often 60 to 70 feet in height and gaily decorated with paper and tinsel canopies is constructed and placed over the corpse and the funeral pyre kindled beneath the structure, which is consumed along with the body. After the cremation, the calcined bones and ashes are collected and buried close to a temple or a *stūpa*. Sometimes, instead of burying the bones, they are collected and pounded into fine powder, which is mixed into a stiff paste and modelled into an image of the Buddha.

In India, the Jains and Bānts (high caste Hindus) of South Kanara, and the Kōtas and Badagas of the Nīlgiris all follow the same custom and erect temporary wooden pagodas over their dead. The Kōtas are low caste Hindus who act as the blacksmiths and musicians to the other hill tribes inhabiting the Nīlgiris. They are a very ancient tribe, and they were living in the Nīlgiris long before the arrival of the Badagas from the plains.

When a Kōta dies, messengers are despatched to the neighbouring Kōta villages to announce the fact, while other members of the caste attend to the construction of a lofty funeral-car. Meanwhile the corpse is dressed in holiday clothes and laid out on a wooden cot inside the house of the deceased, outside which the villagers mourn to the dirge-like strains of a Kōta band. As soon as the funeral-car is completed, it is deposited in front of the house and the corpse brought out on the cot and placed beneath the lowest canopy of the car. The friends and relations wail and lament round the corpse, salute it, and then dance round the car to the accompaniment of Kōta music. Near the head of the corpse are placed a few iron implements and a bag of grain, and beneath the cot, small pots or baskets of grain and other foodstuffs for the use of the dead in the next world. The mourning and dancing proceed for some hours. At length the cot and the car are carried away to the cremation ground, which is situated outside the village and always near a stream and a small wood. On arrival at the selected spot, a few agile Kōtas climb up the wooden scaffolding of the car and remove the umbrellas and cloth canopies for future use. The denuded car is then placed over the corpse, which, deprived of all its finery is placed on the funeral pyre. Around the car faggots of wood, supplied in lieu of wreaths by relations and friends as a mark of respect, are piled up and the pyre lighted. As soon as the pyre and the car are in a blaze, small gifts of tobacco, cloths and grain are usually distributed among those present, and the funeral party disperses. On the following day the ashes are collected and buried in a pit, the spot being marked with a small heap of stones.

A good example of a Kōta funeral-car is shown in Fig. 5. They are built of wood, and consist of a high wooden scaffolding of several storeys In this example the first three storeys are covered with cloth canopies square in shape, decorated with yellow flounces simulating gilt fringes. above these three canopies is a big gourd-like object stuffed with straw and covered with a coloured cloth, which perhaps is meant to represent a Hindu *āmalaka*, the usual ornament which crowns the temples of Northern India. This curious object is surmounted by a large ceremonial umbrella of the usual kind and adorned with a hanging fringe. The small umbrellas fixed above the latter represent a modern innovation Long white streamers hang from the corners of the superimposed canopies, which are built round a single tall pole, while the lowest canopy which overshadows the corpse is supported on four poles planted in the ground and forms a baldachin, or *pandal* as it is called in Southern India, a very important structure in religious and state ceremonial, rivalling that of the umbrella in this respect.

One usually associates Car-Festivals solely with Hindu temples, and the temple of Jagannāth (Vishṇu) at Puri in particular, but in early times the Buddhists, too, held these festivals every year in the Spring, and the Chinese pilgrim Fa Hian has left us a glowing account of them. On his way to India, Fa Hian passed through Khotan (*circa* 400 A.D.), and it was here where he witnessed a Buddhist car-festival. The king of Khotan who was a strong supporter of Buddhism, lodged Fa Hian in a monastery called, Gōmati, where he remained for three months, partly with the object of seeing this important Spring festival for himself. He says [1] "From the first day of the fourth month they sweep and water the roads within the city and decorate the streets. Above the city gate they stretch a great awning and use every kind of adornment. This is where the king and the queen and court ladies take their place. The Gōmati priests, as they belong to the Great Vehicle, which is principally honoured by the king, first of all take their images in procession. About three or four *li* from the city they make a four-wheeled image-car about 30 feet high, in appearance like a moving palace, adorned with the seven precious substances. They fix upon it streamers of silk and canopy curtains (*i.e.*, canopies covered with cloth). The image of the Buddha is placed in the car with two Bodhisattvas as companions, whilst the *devas* (gods) attend on them ; all kinds of polished ornaments made of gold and silver hang suspended in the air. When the image is a hundred paces from the gate, the king takes off his royal cap, and changing his clothes for new ones, proceeds barefooted, with flowers and incense in his hand, from the city, followed by his attendants. On meeting the image he bows down his head and worships at its feet, scattering the flowers and burning the incense. On (the cars) entering the city, the queen and court ladies from above the gate-tower scatter about all kinds of flowers and throw them down in wild profusion. So splendid are the arrangements for worship. The cars are all different, and each *saṅghārāma* (*i.e.*, monastery) has a day (set apart) for its image-procession. They begin on the first day of the fourth month and go on to the fourteenth day, when the processions end. The processions ended, the king and queen then return to the palace."

That these car-processions were general throughout India at the time of Fa Hian's visit seems certain, because when he reached the ancient city of Pātaliputra, now the modern town of Patna in Bihār, he had the

---

[1] Beal's *Buddhist Records of the Western World.* Intro., p. xxvi.

good fortune to witness another of these Buddhist festivals which he describes as follows :—" Every year on the eighth day of the second month there is a procession of images. On this occasion they construct a four-wheeled car, and erect upon it a tower of five stages, composed of bamboos lashed together, the whole being supported by a centre-post resembling a large spear with three points (*trisūla*), in height 22 feet and more. So it looks like a pagoda. They then cover it over with fine white linen, which they afterwards paint with gaudy colours. Having made figures of the *devas*, and decorated them with gold, silver, and glass, they place them under canopies (*i.e.*, umbrellas) of embroidered silk. Then at the four corners (of the car) they construct niches (shrines), in which they place figures of Buddha in a sitting posture, with a Bōdhisattva standing in attendance. There are perhaps twenty cars thus prepared and differently decorated. During the day of the procession both priests and laymen assemble in great numbers. There are games and music, whilst they offer flowers and incense. The Buddhas (*i.e.*, the images in the cars) then, one after the other, enter the city (where) they halt. Then all night long they burn lamps, indulge in games and music, and make religious offerings."[1] From this description we may presume that the festival-cars of ancient India were similar in style and construction to those existing to-day. Fa Hian's remark, that the cars looked like pagodas, is interesting as it indicates that in the fifth century A.D., the temples of India were storeyed wooden buildings similar to the existing pagodas of China and Japan.

Modern festival-cars are temporary wooden structures decorated with coloured cloths and streamers and designed to simulate the stone temples to which they belong. The substructure is strongly built of wood, and is usually richly carved. The four wheels are often of solid stone, and sometimes measure 6 feet in diameter. The cornice of the more important cars is often ornamented with a row of metal bells. This portion of the car is a permanent structure, but the superstructure is a temporary wooden scaffolding covered with coloured cloths specially made for the purpose and surmounted by a big ceremonial umbrella (Fig. 6). In this example, the car simulates a South Indian Temple with a triple-terraced roof. This temporary shrine contains a wooden pedestal, on which the metal image is fixed, and a doorway in front, on each side of which is a painted figure of a doorkeeper with a club. The tubular streamers hanging from the roof all round the car appear to be in imitation of temple pillars, which are often painted with red and white bands at festival times. The cars are dragged in procession by means of strong

[1] *Loc. cit.*, pp. lvi.-lvii.

cables attached to the axle-trees. The car illustrated here is a fine specimen and is richly carved, and belongs to a wealthy temple. Those belonging to the poorer temples are very humble structures, no better than the Kōta funeral-car shown in Fig. 5. In fact, the only real difference between the two is that one has wheels and the other has not; and it seems that in early times also there was very little difference between the two types of cars, as may be gathered from the accounts left us by the Chinese pilgrims cited above.

A number of curious rock-cut tombs have been discovered on the West Coast of India from time to time, and these I shall describe here, as they seem to be intimately connected with our present purpose. The tombs are always discovered by accident, usually by workmen engaged in quarrying the soft laterite stone peculiar to that part of India. They exist in the Chirakkal and Calicut Taluks of Malabar and in several other places on the West Coast. The tombs are excavated out of the rock, circular on plan, with a domed roof supported by a thick round monolithic pillar. The pillar tapers from the top to the bottom, a most unusual feature, resembling in this respect the pillars in the Palace of the Minoan Kings at Cnossos in Crete. The example shown in Fig. 7 was discovered at Chevayur, a village about 5 miles inland from Calicut, and I inspected the tomb a few days after its discovery in 1911. A few feet below the ground, which is of laterite rock, the quarrymen came across the roof of the tomb by accident. The entrance had been carefully closed with blocks of stone so that there was nothing above to indicate that the tomb existed below. On clearing the entrance, which faces the west, the sepulchre was found to consist of a small round cell with a domed roof supported in the centre by a rock-cut pillar. Standing on the floor were twenty-five wheel-made red earthenware cinerary urns and domestic vessels. The larger urns were similar to the big one shown in Fig. 13, and provided with four little legs, while others had pointed bases inserted in pottery ring-stands to enable them to stand upright. The food and water pots were similar to the smaller vessels shown in Fig. 13, types which are common at the present day. In some of these tombs, iron implements and weapons have been found showing that they belong to the Early Iron Age. This tomb appears from the contents found in it to have been a family sepulchre, designed to represent a large umbrella 7 feet 6 inches in diameter overshadowing and protecting the relics of dead ancestors, perhaps those of some local chief.

Another type of tomb found in the same district, also excavated out of the laterite rock, is the Kōda-kallu (Umbrella-stone), so called on account of the big monolithic umbrella-shaped stone which closes the entrance into the sepulchre (Fig. 8). This kind of tomb consists of a small chamber cut out of the laterite and big enough to admit a large pyriform red earthenware urn about 5 feet high and 4 feet wide, the mouth of which is closed with a rounded stone. This urn takes the place of a coffin or sarcophagus, and contains a number of cinerary urns and domestic vessels similar to those described. The Kōda-kallu or circular covering slab rests on the natural ground and measures from 6 to 7 feet in diameter and about 2 feet in thickness, and is monolithic. Its diameter is thus about the same as that of the rock-cut tomb at Chevayur. This great stone not only closes the entrance to the sepulchre, but, being cut in the form of an honorific umbrella canopy, it serves the double purpose of protecting and honouring the dead at the same time.

The occurrence of these massive half-baked earthenware urns in the excavated chambers of the Kōda-kallu seems to supply the necessary link between society, ancient and modern ; for the Malayālīs still adhere to the practice of using small cinerary urns, but in these days the calcined bones of the dead are placed in the urns as a temporary resting-place only, and are, as soon as convenient, removed and cast into some holy river. Formerly there seems to have been no intention of ever disturbing the relics after they were put into the family sepulchre. The shape of some of these urns perhaps affords a clue to the idea which originally suggested this mode of burial. In some specimens the bottom of the urn thickens out in a circular shape, and through this protuberance a small hole is drilled. It has been suggested that this peculiarity in construction is emblematic of the religious ideas connected with the Earth Goddess (*Tellus*), and that burial in this fashion was emblematic of the return of the individual to the womb of Mother Earth.

The worship of the Earth Goddess probably came in with the advance in civilization, which taught men that the earth was fruitful if tilled, and possibly the transition from the excavated tomb period to the age when the burial-urns began to be used marks a change from a pastoral life to one of agriculture, and from a belief in the powers for good and evil of the spirits of the dead to one in which this belief began to be modified by the idea of an Earth Goddess, who became the refuge of the dead.

Besides the Kōda-kallu tombs just mentioned, there is yet another kind of umbrella monument found on the West Coast which belongs to the same early period and is intimately connected with the former.

It is also known locally as a Kōda-kallu, owing to its resemblance to a crudely executed stone model of a ceremonial umbrella (Fig. 9). These monuments are found in small groups, usually erected on sheet rock outside the villages, and often on rising ground, and from a distance resemble a crop of giant mushrooms. The stone canopy is similar in shape and size to that of the last example, but, instead of resting on the ground, it is raised on a roughly hewn laterite pillar about 4 feet high. As nothing has been found beneath these monuments, it is obvious that they are not tombs, but memorials to the dead, probably erected to mark the spot where the body was cremated. Cremation and burial grounds are always located outside the towns and villages, usually on some piece of waste land strictly reserved for the purpose. The old Jain chiefs of South Kanara each had their own private cremation ground known as the *Bakimar* (the field at the gate), because these fields were usually situated in front of the entrance to the chief's palace. Plenty of such fields still exist, and will be referred to again later on.

At a much later date, when the masons of Southern India were more skilled in the art of stone carving, we find these memorial umbrellas really imposing monuments with a quiet dignity of their own, as at Gāvipuram near Bangalore (Fig. 10). The history of this quaint monument is unknown, but we may presume that it was erected in the middle ages in honour of some local chief, or an important religious head, whose body was cremated near the spot. Several stone umbrellas of this kind exist in the neighbourhood of Bangalore set up in temple courtyards, similar specimens are also met with in Burma. It seems probable that the first umbrellas set up as memorials to the dead were of wood, and that it was their perishable nature which led to the idea of executing them in stone as permanent memorials. But even when of stone, the ease with which such top-heavy monuments could be wantonly or accidentally destroyed explains why so few specimens remain.

These primitive memorials to the dead show what a profound influence the umbrella motif had over the religious life of the people of pre-Buddhist India, so it is not surprising to find that in later times, it had a remarkable effect on the evolution of the architecture of that country as we shall see in the following pages.

CHAPTER II.

The Evolution of the Stūpa.

THE commonest kind of ancient sepulchre found in Southern India and the Deccan is the tumulus, the prototype of the Buddhist *stūpa* or tomb. These tumuli are low circular mounds of earth surrounded by a ring of big boulders firmly planted in the ground to keep the tumulus in position and to mark the sacred spot (Fig. 11). Occasionally there is an outer circle of stones around the cairn enclosing a processional path and sacred precinct. The tumuli are either chambered or unchambered. The former contain a large or small rectangular chamber built of roughly hewn slabs of granite, arranged like the sides and ends of a box (Fig. 12). A single slab forms the lid or roof, and when opened they yield a number of wheel-made pottery vessels and cinerary urns like those already described (Fig. 13). Sometimes the front slab of the tomb, which usually faces the east, has a round hole about 9 inches in diameter cut through the centre of the slab, or, instead of this small opening, the front is provided with a small stone-lined passage leading into the tomb, the entrance being closed with a stone slab securely fixed in the ground. The smaller chambers appear to be the graves of single persons, while the large chambers with the openings in front represent family vaults, and as members of the family died, their cremated remains were placed in urns which were passed through the openings, which were promptly closed again. It is impossible to believe that these massively built chambers were opened on each successive occasion of a death, as the labour of opening one from top to bottom would be almost equal to the construction of a new tomb.

The unchambered tumuli have only a floor of stone slabs about 6 feet below the ground, or no floor at all. On this the remains of the dead together with the usual offerings were deposited and covered with earth. Then, as a rule, two or three big heavy blocks of stone were placed on top of the remains, presumably to prevent the spirits of the dead from returning to earth and causing trouble to the living. It seems that these massively built megalithic graves were the outcome of an intense fear of the evil spirits of the dead, rather than to a feeling of affection for the departed, a fear which still survives among all primitive tribes in India at the present day.

Primitive tumuli of this kind existed in India long before the advent of Buddhism and they are not peculiar to any particular caste or community, but it was however, the Buddhists who developed this type of tomb on lines of their own until at last it became the main feature of their architecture.

The chief purpose for which *stūpas* were erected by the Buddhists was to serve as monuments enclosing relics of the Buddha, or of Buddhist saints, which were placed in a reliquary enclosed in a stone coffer, over which the *stūpa* was built. Some, however, contained no relics, but were merely commemorative of important events in the Buddha's life. When they contained relics, the shrine was known as a Dhātugarbha (Pali, *dhatugabho ;* Sinhalese, *dāgaba) ;* and as most *stūpas* were erected over relics (*dhātu*), the whole structure came to be called a Dāgaba. In Tibet they are known as Chortens, and in Northern India, the Anglo-Indian word Tope is usually applied to *stūpas.* At the present day, *stūpa,* tope or *dāgabà,* is a name common to each kind of tumulus, whether it be the solid rock-cut monument dedicated to the Supreme Being, the masonry mound enclosing relics of the Buddha or of Buddhist saints, or the purely memorial *stūpa* erected on some celebrated spot.

The earliest *stūpas* were low circular brick mounds resembling in outline their humble prototypes of the pre-Buddhist period. Thus one of the oldest examples, the brick *stūpa* at Piprahwa on the Nepāl frontier, stands only about 22 feet high, with a basal diameter of 116 feet. As time went on and the building arts progressed, the relative height increased. The well-known Sāñchī Stūpa in Central India, erected much later, is 54 feet high, while the basal diameter is 120 feet, the proportional height here is just about half, while at Piprahwa it is less than one-fifth. In this manner the age of a *stūpa* may be determined approximately from its shape and height, the earliest being a simple hemisphere, and the latest a lofty round brick tower standing on a high terraced platform.

The famous *stūpas* of Bharhut, Sāñchī and Amarāvati have been so often described and illustrated by different writers on Indian art, that one is apt to regard these once magnificent Buddhist shrines as typical examples of *stūpas ;* but as a matter of fact, *stūpas* of this class were the exception. Most of the *stūpas* erected during the reign of the great Asoka (273 to 242 B.C.) were very humble little brick and plaster structures surrounded by a wooden railing with open gateways facing the cardinal points. A good description of early *stūpas* of this kind will be found in General Cunningham's book, *The Bhilsa Topes,* and the following account of the little Andhēr Stūpa is taken from that work. I have selected this monument in particular as its age is known with some degree of certainty. It is built in the usual early form of a bare hemisphere resting on a low circular platform 23 feet in diameter and 3 feet 9 inches in height. The *stūpa* itself is only 15 feet in diameter and was originally about 17 feet high (Fig. 14). On the east side, a double flight of steps gives access to the top of the platform which probably served as a processional path. General Cunningham sank a shaft down the centre of the dome and found a small stone coffer below. This little relic chamber was only 14 inches square and the same in height and built of stone slabs placed so as to overlap at the ends, thus forming a swastika or mystic cross on plan (Fig. 14). Inside the chamber was a small red earthenware urn covered with a lid containing a small steatite reliquary filled with fragments of calcined bone. On the outside of the reliquary is engraved the following inscription—" Relics of the emancipated Hāritiputra ". It is known that this Hāritiputra was one of the principal Buddhist teachers during the reign of Asoka, so the age of this interesting little monument can, therefore, be fixed with more or less certainty. It is interesting to note how closely the construction of the relic chamber resembles that of the stone coffers found in the chambered tumuli of the pre-Buddhist period. The *stūpas* erected over the remains of ordinary members of the Buddhist community were very humble little structures. The ashes of the dead were placed in an earthenware pot and covered with a lid, and the humble little *stūpa* erected over it. Plenty of Buddhist *stūpas* of this class may still be seen in the Madras Presidency and also in Ceylon.

As all the early structural *stūpas* in India are in ruins, most of them having been destroyed by seekers after treasure, we have to fall back on sculptural representations of them in order to form a correct idea of their appearance when complete ; fortunately, we have plenty of material for this purpose. A good example is shown in Fig. 15, a bas-relief from one of the Sāñchī gateways. Here, the *stūpa* represents a small structure similar to the Andhēr example. It represents a brick *stūpa* covered with plaster standing on a low circular drum and surrounded by the usual wooden railing. Half way up the dome is a row of horn-like wooden pegs driven into the face of the brickwork so as to serve as supports for the garlands festooned round the dome. Most *stūpas* seem to have been decorated in this manner, originally with garlands of fresh flowers, the gifts of pious devotees, but in later times the garland became a conventional architectural ornament executed in plaster, and the row of pegs, being no longer necessary, disappeared. The four human figures portrayed standing round the base of the monument represent worshippers, while on the left is a king with his umbrella-bearer behind him seated on an elephant, apparently just arrived at the holy shrine and about to dismount from the elephant. Above the *stūpa* two winged cherubs are depicted bringing garlands to decorate the summit of the shrine. The curious simulated wooden structure surmounting the *stūpa* is known to Indian archæologists as the 'tee', an Anglicised form of the Burmese word *hti*, by which this member is now generally known.

The tee has disappeared from all the structural *stūpas* in India, but its form may be seen from *stūpas* surviving in Ceylon and Burma, as well as from stone models and sculptural representations preserved in great numbers in India. The box-like nature of construction depicted in these carved representations of tees, and the fact that all the structural tees have perished, presumably destroyed by treasure-seekers when Buddhism declined in India, indicates that originally they were wooden coffers or receptacles for valuable offerings presented to the shrine by pious worshippers. The four sides of the tee are usually decorated with the rail ornament, a sure indication of a simulated wooden structure, while the lid of the tee is portrayed as consisting of two or three superimposed slabs of wood or stone (Fig. 15).

In all these sculptural representations of *stūpas* the tee is always shown surmounted by an umbrella, or a group of umbrellas, to which banners or streamers are sometimes added. This umbrella finial was known in ancient India as the *chhatrāvali*, while in Burma it is called a *hti* as mentioned above. The installation of this architectural member was, and still is, a very important and often costly religious ceremony, because before the *chhatrāvali* was fixed in position on the summit of a *stūpa*, or a temple, valuable offerings in the form of gold coins or jewels were placed beneath it and built into its foundations. The Brāhmans followed the same custom when installing a *kalasa*, or gilt-copper finial, on the summit of their temples. As this custom still prevails and is well known in India, whenever a *stūpa* or a temple fell into disuse, thieves immediately removed these crowning ornaments and stole the offerings placed beneath them. This is one of the chief reasons why all the structural tees have disappeared in India, and also explains why so many ancient Hindu temples, no longer used for worship, are minus their *kalasas*.

In the Sinhalese chronicle, the *Mahāvaṁsa*, we have a graphic account of the building and dedication of the Mahāthūpa (Great Stūpa) in Ceylon, in the reign of King Duṭṭhagāmaṇī (*circa* 101 to 77 B.C.), to enshrine a relic of the Buddha obtained from India. From this account we learn that the foundations of this *stūpa* were of rough stone trodden down by elephants, and on this foundation the brick *stūpa* was built. The relic chamber was formed of six slabs of stone and faced the east. One slab was placed flat and formed the floor of the chamber, four were arranged like the sides of a box, and the sixth was the lid. The construction of the relic chamber was thus, similar in all respects to the stone-built chamber illustrated in Fig. 12, and it must have been quite as large, as the account mentions the king " stepping down into it." The Buddha relics, which were in a golden casket, were placed in the chamber by the king himself, who also made an offering of all the royal ornaments on his person, his ministers and others in attendance doing likewise. After the dedication ceremony was over, the brick dome was built over the relic chamber. The king then dedicated his state umbrella to the *stūpa*, exclaiming with joy : "Thrice over do I dedicate my kingdom to the redeemer of the world, the divine teacher, the bearer of the triple canopy, the canopy of the heavenly host, the canopy of mortals, and the canopy of eternal emancipation." The king then permitted his royal umbrella to remain on the summit of the *stūpa* for seven days, when it was subsequently replaced by a stone or wooden model of the same. At this time, when only the plastering of the dome and the fixing of the permanent umbrella on top of the tee remained to be done, the king fell sick, and as he was on the point of death he enjoined his young brother Tissa to complete the great work. We are told that Tissa quickly covered the dome of the *stūpa* with a white cloth so as to resemble plaster, and raised a cloth umbrella with a bamboo staff on top of the tee ; and then announced to the king that the *stūpa* was finished. The dying monarch was carried to the spot and laid on a carpet opposite the southern entrance, where, after gazing with delight on the holy shrine, he breathed his last. The *stūpa* was completed by Tissa, who succeeded him on the throne of Ceylon. It is also recorded that between the years 79 and 89 A.D., the Rāja Amaṇḍagāmanī erected another umbrella on the tee of the *Mahāthūpa*, and lastly, Rāja Sirināga, between 249 and 268 A.D., gilded the two umbrella canopies of the Great Stūpa. It is clear from this description of the building and dedication of the *Mahāthūpa* in Ceylon, how these state umbrellas came to be connected with the early *stūpas*.

In all probability, it was during the reign of Asoka, after he made Buddhism the religion of the State, that the royal umbrella first became associated with the *stūpa* in India. These emblems of sovereignty are portrayed in the bas-reliefs and stone models as fixed to the lid of the tee in such a manner as made it impossible for anyone to open or tamper with the tee without first removing the umbrella. In this manner the umbrella seems to have been a means of proclaiming to the public that the *stūpas* were under the protection of the State.

All important *stūpas* were provided with wooden railings (*vedikā*), and gateways (*toraṇa*) at the four cardinal points enclosing a processional path around the shrine. Of the existing specimens, the best known are those belonging to the Sāñchī Stūpa in Bhopāl State. Ordinarily the railings and gateways were of wood, but where durability was considered of paramount importance, these wooden structures were occasionally copied in stone, probably by royal command (Figs 16 and 17).

The gateways, which are generally called by the Sanskrit name *toraṇa*, were introduced into China and Japan along with other forms of Buddhist architecture from India. In China, under the name of *pailoos*, they are frequently constructed in wood; when made of stone they retain down to the present day the forms and details of timber construction like the *toraṇas* at Sāñchī. A very interesting fact in the history of this architectural member is that these *pailoos* are still used in China as gateways to indicate tombs, just as their prototypes the *toraṇas* were used in India two thousand years ago.

Buddhist architecture was introduced into Japan by way of Korea in the seventh century A.D., and there is little doubt that the Japanese *tori* gates, like the *pailoos* which they closely resemble, are the lineal descendants of the Indian *toraṇas*. There are similar wooden gateways in Korea.

Asoka is credited with the construction, all over Northern India, of a large number of *stūpas* enshrining relics of the Buddha or Buddhist saints; and with them were erected monasteries or *vihāras* for the monks. We cannot positively identify any of the few still existing *stūpas* as having been actually built by him; but there is no doubt that the Bharhut and Sāñchī stūpas, the carved railing at Bodh-Gayā, the Barābar caves, and the oldest of the rock-cut temples and *vihāras* in Western India, were excavated during the existence of the Maurya dynasty, or at least within the two centuries following Aśoka's accession.

It was thus partly, at least, to Buddhism, under the impulse of this powerful and enlightened sovereign, that we owe the inception of all the monuments that have come down to us from that age. Buddhism

5——J. N. 55882 (6/36)

had not then developed the cult of a personal Buddha farther than to reverence his relics, the representation of his footprints, the sacred Bodhi-tree and other symbols, combined with aboriginal tree and serpent worship. But we must not forget, however, that the Jains and other sects, contemporary with the Buddhists, were also protected by this beneficent monarch, and that they built *stūpas* and excavated rock-cut shrines and monastic abodes for their devotees, and further that these are now recognized by distinctive symbols, by inscriptions or by other evidence of the sects for whom they were excavated.

The *stūpas* at Sāñchī are one of several groups of such monuments situated within a few miles of Bhīlsa on the G. I. P. Railway in Bhopāl State, and commonly known as the Bhīlsa Topes.[1] One of these groups is on the hill above Sonārī ; another at Sātdhārā ; a third at Bhojpur ; and a fourth at Andhēr. Their existence in the vicinity of Bhīlsa is not due to mere chance. It is explained by the fact that near the modern town and at the junction of the Bes and Betwā rivers there once stood the famous and populous city of Vidisā, and that around this city there grew up a flourishing community of Buddhists, who found on the summits of the neighbouring hills suitable sites for erecting their memorials and monasteries. In the case of other famous Buddhist monuments, such as those at Bodh-Gayā, Sārnāth or Sankīsā, the sites were chosen because they had become hallowed by the presence of the Buddha himself, and the monuments were designed to commemorate some act in his life, such as his attainment of enlightenment at Bodh-Gayā, his first sermon at Sārnāth, and his passing away at Kasiā. But Sāñchī so far as we know, had no such connection with the life or acts of the Great Teacher, and the place is scarcely mentioned in Buddhist literature. It is a strange coincidence, therefore, that these monuments should now be the finest examples of this style of Buddhist architecture in India. In all probability it was their association with Asoka, who was to Buddhism what Constantine the Great was to Christianity, that accounts for the splendour of these structures. For one of the queens of Asoka, Devī by name, came from Vidisā ; and it was on the hill of Sāñchī, then known as Chetiyagiri, that a monastery is said to have been built for his son Mahendra. Whether this story is correct or not, the fact remains that the earliest monuments here belong to the reign of this great monarch, as is proved by the broken shaft and lion capital of one of his famous edict-bearing pillars still standing outside the southern gateway of the Great Stūpa at Sāñchī.

---

[1] See *The Bhilsa Topes*, by General Cunningham.

It has commonly been supposed that the Great Stūpa was erected, just as it stands, together with the inscribed pillar outside the southern gateway, in the reign of Asoka, and that the railing around its base was approximately contemporary with the *stūpa*, and that the four *toraṇas* were erected in the course of the second century B.C. These suppositions, however, as pointed out by Sir John Marshall in his excellent *Guide to Sāñchī*, have proved to be erroneous. The original *stūpa*, which was probably built by Asoka at the same time as his edict-bearing pillar was erected (*circa* 250 B.C.), was a brick structure of about half the height and diameter of the present *stūpa*, and it was not until about a century later, during the Suṅga period, that this original brick structure was encased in a covering of stone which brought the *stūpa* to its present dimensions, and the stone railing was built around its base; while it was not until the latter part of the first century B.C. that the four gateways were added.

With the addition of the stone casing the diameter of the *stūpa* was increased to over 120 feet and its height to about 54 feet. This later casing to the dome was built of stone covered by a thick coating of mortar, finished off in plaster and a stucco garland ornament around the dome relieved with colour and gilding.

The last of the additions to this remarkable monument were the elaborate and richly carved gateways. The style and construction of both the rails and the gateways clearly shows that they are stone copies of former wooden models, and in all probability, the original railings and *toraṇas* enclosing the brick *stūpa* built by Asoka were executed in wood, just as we find them in China and Japan at the present day. All four gateways were of similar design—the work of carpenters rather than stone masons, and the marvel is that erections of this kind, constructed on principles wholly unsuited to work in stone, should have survived in such a remarkable state of preservation for nearly two thousand years. According to their age, the *toraṇas* stand in the following order—the southern, northern, eastern, and the western, their relative age in each case being indicated by inscriptions and the styles of their sculpture. The latter exhibit a great advance in the modelling of figures and minuteness of detail, and in many other respects also art begins to profit by the direct observation of nature. Here and there, the sculpture of the Suṅga period at Sāñchī, as well as at Bharhut and Bodh-Gayā, reveal the influence which Hellenistic ideas exerted on Indian Art through the medium of the contemporary Greek colonies in the Panjāb, although the character of these reliefs and their wonderful sense of decorative beauty are essentially Indian.

In the beautiful Sāñchī bas-reliefs we have many representations of *stūpas* surmounted by single-, double-, and triple-canopied umbrellas, together with superimposed groups of umbrellas numbering from three to five, but they have not as yet been conventionalized so as to produce the pyramid of superimposed discs which subsequently came to be recognized as the symbol of the whole. Thus we have the primary idea of the accumulated honour of the pyramid of stone or metal discs, which eventually had such a profound influence on Buddhist architecture, culminating in the many-storeyed pagodas of China and Japan.

The only ancient wooden umbrella existing in India to-day is the well-known example crowning the rock-cut *stūpa* in the Kārlē Chaitya in the Bombay Presidency; but stone specimens are common. Ancient metal umbrellas are rare in India now, but they seem to have been common enough in the seventh century, as Hiuen Tsang expressly states that several of the *stūpas* and *vihāras* which he visited were surmounted by superimposed copper-gilt *chhatras* (umbrellas). The umbrellas portrayed in the Sāñchī reliefs appear to represent wooden umbrellas similar to the one remaining at Kārlē, as it would have been impossible to have grouped them together in the manner depicted had they been of stone. The latter material seems to have been used only for single-canopied umbrellas and rock-cut specimens.

Although the structural umbrellas, like the tees, which together crowned the early *stūpas* have all disappeared, we still have plenty of rock-cut examples and stone models of *stūpas*, illustrating the successive stages through which these conventionalized groups of umbrellas passed before assuming the form of a solid stone spire.

The different stages of development are well shown in the chronologically successive rock-cut specimens and stone models illustrated in Figs 18 to 21. It will be noticed that, concurrently with the elongation of the tee, there is also an elongation of the body of the *stūpa*, until finally we arrive at the last development where the tee is practically all that is left. Another striking feature in the development of the *stūpa*, as shown in these illustrations, is that figure sculpture has superseded the plainer architectural forms of the earlier *stūpas*, and that the Buddha has now been introduced in all his conventional attitudes and is even the object of worship, his image being placed in a shrine attached to the front of the *stūpa* (Fig. 20).

The rock-cut *stūpa* shown in Fig. 18, is from Kānheri in the Bombay Presidency, and is an early example. It is circular on plan, low in proportion to its height, and free from ornament. The umbrella is of the plain wheel-like type portrayed in the Sāñchī sculptures. It stands in a little shrine chamber hewn out of the natural rock. The hole shown in its side represents the work of treasure-seekers. The next example (Fig. 19) is from Dhamnār in the Indore State, Central India. A description of the Dhamnār monuments will be found in Volume II of Cunningham's Reports. It stands in a small rock-cut temple measuring 23½ feet in length and 15 feet in width. The vaulted roof of the shrine is ribbed in imitation of a wooden structure. The *stūpa* itself, which is also carved out of the natural rock, is 16½ feet in height and stands on a square base 9½ feet in width. The body of the *stūpa* is similar but higher than the last example. The tee itself is of normal shape, but the double-canopied umbrella decorated with the lotus ornament is a new departure not met with before. Owing to the absence of inscriptions, the age of the Dhamnār excavations is a little difficult to determine. But from the lofty form of this *stūpa*, its square base and style of its umbrella, it may probably be assigned to the sixth century A.D.

The combined elongation of the *stūpa* and the tee is well represented in Fig. 20, a late specimen from Cave No. 19 at Ajanta. Here the low hemisphere of the Asokan age has become conventionalized into a lofty ornamental tower surmounting an elaborately carved base square on plan with doubly-recessed angles. But stranger still is the form the triple-umbrella has assumed. It is now a tall steeple-like object reaching to the roof of the rock-cut shrine in which it stands. Its original form and meaning would hardly be suspected by those who were not familiar with the intermediate steps. The stone canopies of the umbrella are ornamented with the lotus moulding and supported by little figures of *gaṇas*, or dwarfs, while the summit is crowned with a miniature *stūpa* as a finial. Carved on the front face of the *stūpa* and standing under a *makara-toraṇa* is an image of the Buddha as the object of worship. Thus we find that in the seventh century A.D., or thereabouts, the *stūpa* had assumed the shape of a temple, square on plan, with a domed roof surmounted by an ornamental spire. Nor was it in external appearnce only that the *stūpa* had assumed this new form. For among the numerous stone and brick models of small votive *stūpas* erected by pious pilgrims around the great brick temple at Bodh-Gayā, and the Svayambhūnāth Stūpa in Nepāl, we find many examples of *stūpas* with hollowed-out interiors for the reception of an image of the Buddha (Fig. 22).

When Buddhist pilgrims visited any of the famous sites connected with the life of their Great Teacher, it was their invariable custom to make some offering, no matter how poor, to the shrine, and at the same time set up some memorial of their visit. These offerings consisted of money, jewels, and other costly articles by the rich, and of fruit and flowers by the poor. The memorials usually took the form of *stūpas* and temples of all sizes by the wealthy, and of small stone models of *stūpas* and temples, or inscribed clay tablets by the poor. There is a great variety in the shape and style of these votive *stūpas* as may be seen in Fig. 22, from the low hemisphere to the tall ornamental spire surmounting the medieval dome, with ornamental square base. In these later examples we find figures of the Buddha placed in decorated niches on each side of the base.

The Svayambhūnāth Stūpa, near Kāthmaṇḍū, the capital of Nepāl, is dedicated to Svayambhūnāth, the "Self Existent Lord", and is the most popular place of Lamaist pilgrimage outside Tibet. Immense numbers of Tibetans, both Lamas and laity, visit the *stūpa* every winter, and encamp in the surrounding fields for making offerings to the shrine and circumbulating the sacred spot. Its special virtue is reputed to be its power of granting all prayers for wordly wealth, children, and everything else asked for. The *stūpa* stands on the top of a forest-clad hill about a mile to the west of Kāthmaṇḍū, and consists of a solid masonry hemisphere standing on a low circular drum or basement. The dome is about 60 feet in diameter and 30 feet in height. The drum is decorated with a simulated railing around the structure, and built partly into this basement are several large ornamental niches, four of which face the four points of the compass. Each niche thus forms a separate shrine which is plated with copper-gilt and contains an image of the Buddha rather larger than life-size. The four faces of the tee are covered with copper plates, and have a large pair of open eyes, painted in red, white, and black colours on each of the four sides. These eyes denote that the *stūpa* is dedicated to the Adi Buddha, the Divine Spirit who is "Light". Above the four sides of the square tee are four pentagonal plaques, also of copper-gilt, on each face of which are riveted five small metal images of the Dhyānī Buddhas. Surmounting the tee is a huge *chhatrāvali*, consisting of thirteen superimposed wooden umbrella canopies fixed to a single staff. The edge or rim of each canopy is bound with copper and plated with gold. Above this is a large single bell-shaped umbrella of metal representing the highest heaven of the Buddhists.

Unfortunately in India all the later structural examples of *stūpas* are in ruins, the upper portions having decayed and disappeared, but in Ceylon and Burma a few good specimens belonging to this period still survive. As representative of this class of *stūpa*, we may take the Sapada Stūpa at Pagān in Burma (Fig. 23). It was built by a Burmese monk named Sapada who received his ordination in Ceylon and who founded a sect at Pagān in the reign of king Narapatisithu (*c.* 1173–1210 A.D.). It is the prototype of similar *stūpas* in the Province, and is a landmark in the history of Buddhism, as it commemorates the religious intercourse between Burma and Ceylon. It stands on a large brick platform 88 feet square, which is approached by a flight of steps on the eastern and western sides. The steps lead up to a brick and plaster *toraṇa*, but there is not much resemblance between this later type of *toraṇa* and those at Sāñchī. The style shows that the pious monk Sapada took as his model a *stūpa* which he had seen, and doubtless admired, in Ceylon. It will be noticed that the *stūpa* is still round on plan. The base or drum is high, and is ornamented with rows of mouldings. The bell-shaped dome is surmounted by a well-defined square tee while the *chhatrāvali* is represented by a pyramid of discs executed in brick and plaster like those so common in Ceylon.

The last stage in the development of the Burmese *stūpa* is well represented by the Tawyagyaung Stūpa at Mandalay (Fig. 24). Here the *stūpa*, or what is left of it, stands on a high triple-terraced platform built of brick and plaster. The four corners of the base are guarded by stucco figures of leogryphs, while the angles of the terraces are decorated with simulated urns and miniature shrines. This elaborate basement is supposed to represent Mount Meru. In some of these later Burmese examples, and also in those of Siam and Java, the basement is an enormous structure of many terraces one above the other, each decorated with rows of miniature shrines which are grouped round the central *stūpa*. In this example (Fig. 24), the square tee of the earlier *stūpas* has disappeared, its place being taken by an elongated brick and plaster cone decorated with rings which simulate the usual superimposed *chhatras*, above which is an elaborate metal umbrella denoting the highest Buddhist Heaven.

The metal *chhatrāvalis* of ancient India consisted of a tall iron rod supporting a number of copper-gilt *chhatras*, usually nine or thirteen, and the *chhatras* were often adorned with little metal bells. This is the usual form of terminal to most religious buildings of importance in many Buddhist lands at the present day. It is no longer met with in

India, but there is evidence to show that it was a common object in the seventh century, and probably long before that date. Several representations of this member, in stone and in metal, have been recovered from Gandhāra dating back to the third century A.D.

The Chinese pilgrim Sung Yun (518 A.D.) has left us a good description of a wooden Buddhist temple which he saw in Peshāwar, in those days the centre of Buddhism in Northern India. He calls this building the *Tsioh-li-feou-thou* (a pagoda with a surmounting rod). He states that throughout the building the king used carved wood and constructed stairs leading to the top of the building, which was thirteen storeys in height. The roof was of wood and surmounted by an iron rod, 30 feet high and decorated with thirteen (superimposed) gilded *chhatras* (umbrellas). (*See* Beal's *Buddhist Records of the Western World, Vol. I.*, p. civ.) Hwei Sang, a brother pilgrim who accompanied Sung Yun to Peshāwar, was so impressed by the beauty and dignity of the *Tsioh-li* temple that he employed a skilful artist to depict the *Tsioh-li* pagoda and the four principal *stūpas* of the Buddha on copper. These engravings on copper (or perhaps models in copper) were taken back to China by the pilgrims, where no doubt they served as models for Buddhist temples and *stūpas* erected in that country. Sung Yun informs us that the *Tsioh-li* temple since its first erection by king Kanishka, was thrice struck by lightning, but each time the ruling king restored it. No doubt the metal *chhatrāvali* surmounting the structure was the cause of its destruction. If the *Tsioh-li* pagoda was thrice destroyed by lightning, we may be sure many other buildings surmounted by these metal finials shared a similar fate, which, to some extent, may explain why they have all disappeared. Metal *chhatrāvalis* seem to have been common enough in the seventh century when Hiuen Tsang visited India, as he repeatedly mentions them as adorning the Buddhist buildings, not only *stūpas,* but temples and monasteries of wooden construction. He also informs us that some of these buildings were destroyed by fire, perhaps caused by lightning, though he does not expressly say so. However, if we have no examples of metal *chhatrāvalis* in India to-day, we have plenty of stone models belonging to the later Buddhist period portraying them.

A good example is shown in Fig. 21, a stone model of a medieval Buddhist *stūpa* discovered at Sārnāth near Benares, and now in the Sārnāth Museum. Its base is square with recessed angles ; the four sides of the drum are provided with niches containing little images of the Buddha as the object of worship. The dome of the *stūpa* has sunk to a very subordinate position, whereas, the tee and umbrellas have assumed the form of a conical spire taller than the *stūpa* itself. The square tee is portrayed with a simulated wooden roof with curved eaves and the ends of the rafters showing at the angles, just as they appear in the widely projecting roofs of the Japanese wooden temples. The obviously wooden treatment of this stone representation of a tee, indicates that the tees were often made of wood, which helps to explain why all the structural tees in India have disappeared. The tee is surmounted by a simulated metal *chhatrāvali* like those still existing in some of the oldest wooden pagodas of Japan. It simulates a tall iron rod decorated with nine superimposed copper-gilt *chhatras*, from which little bells are suspended, the latter being indicated by small triangular stone projections, and, as usual, a larger single *chhatra* crowns the whole and represents the highest Buddhist Heaven.

In early times the *stūpa* was the principal object of worship with the Buddhists, but with the introduction of the Buddha image in the second century A.D., or thereabouts, temples became necessary to enshrine these images, and in course of time, as Buddhism became more and more idolatrous, the temples ousted the *stūpas* as popular places of worship. The Gandhāra sculptures show that by the second or third century a definite type of temple had been adopted by the Northern Buddhists, a building similar in most respects to the Brāhmaṇical fire-temples of Gandhāra at that period, and from which the Buddhist temples appear to have been directly copied. So we cannot credit the Buddhists as being the first people in India to erect temples to their gods, since fire worship is an older religion than Buddhism. However, there is one type of Buddhist temple which seems to be wholly Buddhist in origin, and that is the Burmese Buddhist temple built of brick and plaster.

The Buddhist scriptures reached Burma, and China too, in very early times, but Buddhist architecture and sculpture followed some centuries later. All the earlier Buddhist monuments discovered in Burma resemble the later Buddhist monuments of India, and those of Southern India in particular, and it seems that the chief influence came from that part of India. Kāñchipuram, now the modern town of Conjeeveram in the Madras Presidency, was the ancient capital of the Pallava dynasty from very early times, and in the fifth century was a great centre of the Hīnayāna form of Buddhism. It was the home of Dharmapāla, the great commentator, a contemporary of the famous Buddhaghoṣa of that period. The Pallavas had an important seaport at Māmallapuram, now popularly known as the Seven Pagodas. In all probability it was mainly from this port that the Buddhist architecture of Southern India found its way into Burma and the Far East in the seventh and eighth centuries A.D., thus accounting for the striking resemblance between the earliest monuments of Burma and the later Buddhist buildings of India. It must be remembered that when Buddhism was a new and flourishing religion in Burma, that religion was rapidly waning in India, and by 700 A.D., it had become so idolatrous that it closely resembled Hinduism, until at last it succumbed altogether in face of the revival of that religion, which had absorbed much of the ethical teaching of Buddhism, and had even come to acknowledge the Buddha as one of the ten incarnations of Vishṇu.

Unfortunately in India very few structural Buddhist temples survive, but a few good specimens still remain in Burma and Ceylon to show us what they were like. They are usually built of brick and plaster, and in style and on plan resemble the medieval votive temples to be seen in the enclosures belonging to the Bodh-Gayā temple and the Svayambhūnāth Stūpa (Fig. 22).

The early Burmese temples are square on plan, and contain an image of the Buddha, or a small *stūpa*, as the object of worship. The latter is placed in a cell in the base of the structure and occupies the very same position which the relics of the Buddha occupied in the earliest *stūpas*. An excellent example of this kind of hollow *stūpa* is the Nyaungu temple in Burma (Fig. 25). The brick porch is decorated with a *makara-toraṇa*, a type of arch which originated in Northern India, where it is still met with. The square base of the structure is high, the tee is absent and the bell-shaped body of the *stūpa* is elongated into a tall cone originally divided into nine simulated *chhatras* executed in brick and plaster, and crowned, perhaps, with a metal umbrella finial denoting the highest Heaven.

The next example is a Buddhist temple at Pagān, which contains a small brick *stūpa* as the object of worship (Fig. 26). Here, the basement is no longer a mass of solid brickwork containing a cell pierced in its centre as in the last example, but is a properly constructed square cell with a *toraṇa* entrance on each of its four sides. Surmounting the roof is a high two-storeyed terrace originally decorated with miniature simulated *stūpas* at the corners of each storey. On top of the upper terrace stands a brick and plaster model of a *stūpa*. Here the *stūpa* is purely ornamental and serves no useful purpose whatever, as the object of worship is enshrined in the square cella below. In fact we have now arrived at the stage when the *stūpa* became transformed into a temple. The same thing also happened in India, as may be seen by a glance at the collection of medieval Buddhist shrines built around the great Svayambhūnāth Stūpa (Fig. 22).

The only structural example so far discovered in India showing the transformation of the Buddhist *stūpa* into a temple is the one illustrated in Fig. 27. It was discovered at the great monastery site at Nālandā in Bihār a few years ago by the Archæological Survey of India. It is built of brick and ornamented in stucco, and consists of a medieval *stūpa* square on plan, with a small shrine chamber in front for the reception of an image of the Buddha. A stone model of a similar building was discovered at Bodh-Gayā by General Cunningham and is illustrated in his book *Mahabodhi*, and there is no doubt that Buddhist temples of this kind were common in Bihār in the seventh and eighth centuries. The *chhatrāvali* is missing from the Nālandā example, but, when complete, it was probably in brick and plaster and similar to the one surmounting the Sārnāth example. The trefoil plaques are filled with little seated figures of the Buddha, all except one, which contains a figure of the Buddhist goddess Tārā. Below the rounded mouldings of the dome and the cornice of the lofty square base are rows of modillions. When complete the structure was covered with plaster and the ornamentation was probably picked out in a few simple colours, as in Hindu temples. The style of the base, the modillions and the trefoil plaques suggest Gandhāra influence.

When Buddhism declined in India in the seventh century A.D., and Brāhmaṇism in the form of Hinduism re-asserted itself as the popular religion of the country, there was no longer any demand for Buddhist monuments. The old master-builders and their descendants, who from 250 B.C. to 600 A.D., had been mainly employed in building or excavating monuments for the Jains and Buddhists, were now called upon to erect temples for the Brāhmaṇs. Whatever Brāhmaṇical temples may have been built prior to the seventh century A.D. must have been mainly of wood and have long since perished, as no remains of such buildings have been discovered. So when the Brāhmaṇs started to build their temples of stone, or to carve them out of rock, they had to employ builders who had formerly worked for the Buddhists with the result that many Buddhist features were reproduced in these early Hindu temples. Even in later times, when the Brāhmaṇs of the north and the south of India had each developed a definite style of their own, traces of Buddhist influence are manifest.

As a case in point, let us examine the typical so-called Dravidian Hindu temple of the south (Fig. 28). Temples of this kind, large or small, ancient or modern, may be seen in almost every town or village in the Tamil country. The earliest examples date back to the seventh century, when the Pallavas were ruling in the south, and the latest are quite modern. The temple shown here, is situated at Kambaduru, a village in the Anantapur district of the Madras Presidency, and is dedicated to Siva's consort Pārvatī, and was probably built in the sixteenth century. The shrine consists of the usual square sanctum built of stone with a flat roof of the same material. The latter is surmounted by a brick and plaster structure known in the south as a *stūpi*, a name which is obviously a corruption of the Sanskrit word *stūpa.* If we compare this architectural ornament with the domed roof of the Nālānda temple (Fig. 27), it is clear how it originated and why it is called a *stūpi* at the present day.

Like the Nālānda temple, the figures and ornamentation including the rows of modillions of the *stūpi*, are executed in stucco. In both examples the sides of the dome are decorated with trefoil-shaped plaques, an ornament which originated with the Gandhāra Buddhists in very early times. These striking resemblances between the Buddhist *stūpa* and the Dravidian *stūpi* cannot be due to mere coincidence. Other influences may have helped in producing the Hindu temple of the south, but there is no doubt as to how the *stūpi* which surmounts it originated.

CHAPTER III.

Kerala Architecture.

THE most remarkable feature about the wooden architecture of the West Coast of India, from South Kanara to Travancore, is its striking resemblance to that of the Himalayas. As there is no possibility of the former style influencing that of the latter, we must look for some other reason to account for this strange phenomenon, and the only one which presents itself in this case is a common origin for both styles of architecture. We saw in the last Chapter, how the development of the Buddhist temple was greatly influenced by the umbrella motif, and in this case too, the same religious symbol seems to have been mainly responsible for the peculiar style of wooden temple found in this region, formerly known as Kerala.

Both Jainism and Buddhism arose in India about the same period, and in the same region—Bihār. The Jains erected both *stūpas* and temples, which in style and construction were similar to those of the Buddhists. They paid the same reverence to the umbrella as an emblem of religious sovereignty, and always placed it above their sacred buildings and over the heads of their images, and, what is of still more importance for our purpose, they erected wooden funeral-cars decorated with superimposed canopies and umbrellas over the remains of their dead, a custom which the Jains and Hindus of the West Coast, and the Burmese Buddhists, follow at the present day.

Before attempting a description of the Kerala style of architecture, we will first briefly ascertain what influence Jainism and Buddhism may have had in this part of India in early times. According to the *South Kanara Manual* (Vol. I., pages 187 to 191), Buddhism was introduced into Tuluva (Kanara) as early as 250 B.C. This conclusion appears to be based upon the reference in Asoka's Rock Edict II. to Kerala, the ancient name for the West Coast country, from Kanara to Travancore. In early times there does not appear to have been much difference between Jainism and Buddhism, and such traces as have been found in Western India indicate the prevalence of Jainism rather than Buddhism. The early Kadambas of Banavāsi in North Kanara, and the Chālukyas who succeeded the Pallavas as overlords of Kanara, were undoubtedly Jains, and it is probable that some of the Pallava kings held the same faith. The later Kadambas, who are credited with bringing in the Brāhmaṇs about the eighth century A.D., may or not have been Jains at that time, as there is plenty of evidence to show that early in the Christian era Jains, Saivas and Vaishṇavas lived and worshipped amicably together. From that time there was nothing to interfere with the growth of Brāhmaṇism in Malabar, but in Kanara a check seems to have been administered to Brāhmaṇ power by the transfer of the headquarters of Southern Jainism from Mysore to Kanara not long after the conversion of the Hoysala Ballāla king Vishṇuvardhana to Vaishṇavism about 1137 A.D. The Jain Kadamba chiefs of Humcha in Mysore, then moved their capital to Kārkala in Kanara, where, under the name of Bairasu Woḍeyars, they continued in power under the Vijayanagar kings, until the power of the latter began to decline in the sixteenth century, when these Jain chiefs made a bid for independence, but were overthrown by the Liṅgāyat family of Ikkeri and Bednore in Mysore, who had obtained a grant of the provinces of Bārkūr and Mangalore in Kanara from the Vijayanagar kings. The struggle between the Liṅgāyats and Jains seem to have been fiercest in the north of Kanara, where the last representative of the Bairasu Woḍeyars was in power as queen of Bhatkal, and by 1608 Veṅkaṭappa Nāyak had nearly extirpated the Jains of Bārkūr and reduced to ruins all the Jain temples in that city. Against the Jain chiefs in the Mangalore province, notably Chautar of Mūdabidri and Bangar of Nandavar, he was not so successful, and they were permitted to retain some authority as feudatories until the time of Haidar and Tippu, when they were deprived of the last vestiges of power; though representatives of their families still remain in the possession of a portion of their old private lands and palaces. With the decadence of the political power of the Jains the faith of their adherents began also to wane. It never had any hold on the lower castes, and even the land-holding classes, who are mainly Bānts (Hindus), probably assumed it as a fashionable addition to the ancestral demon-worship to which they all still adhere, whether they profess to be Hindus or Jains. The Jains of to-day are a small class numbering less than ten thousand souls, and residing chiefly at Mūdabidri and Kārkala, the capitals of the most powerful of the old Jain chiefs of South Kanara.

The Jains of Kanara belong to the Digambara, naked or sky-clad, division, and hence their images are represented in the nude. The objects of worship in the Jain temples, or *bastis*, as they are called locally, are the twenty-four Tirthaṅkaras or Siddhas, saints who have become gods, and to any one of whom, besides his own special name, or to all collectively may be given the name Jina, Jinesvara, or Arhat.

In the chief temple at Mūdabidri prominence is given to Chandranātha, the eighth Tirthaṅkara, but the colossal statues at Kārkala and Yenūr are said to represent Gomata Rāya, a mythical hero of whom nothing is really known. The statue at Kārkala is said in an inscription to have been erected in 1432 A.D., to Bāhubali, son of Vṛishabha, the first Tirthaṅkara. The features of the statue are similar to those which are found on the images of the Buddha throughout the Eastern world, and the same features recur in all the representations of the Tirthaṅkaras in the different temples (Fig. 29).

Besides being of colossal size, the Kārkala statue is rendered more striking by its situation on the summit of a rocky hill situated above a picturesque little lake.

The following description of it is quoted in the *South Kanara Manuel*[1] :— " Upon the out-skirts of the town rises a rocky hill of generally rounded from like a basin reversed approaching 300 feet in height, its base rough and bushy, the upper slopes smooth and steep. Looking up the hill from a distance the enchanted castles of fairy tales come back to mind, for on the top is seen a castle-like wall pierced with a wide arched entrance, and a dark gigantic form towering over it waist high. This is one of those colossal statues that are found in this part of the country, statues truly Egyptian in size, and unrivalled throughout India as detached works. On the hill-top a crenelated quadrangular wall encloses a stone platform 4 feet high, on which rises the stupendous image 41 feet in height. Nude, cut from a single mass of granite, darkened by the monsoons of centuries, the vast statue stands upright, with arms hanging straight, but not awkwardly, down the sides, in a position of somewhat stiff but simple dignity. Remarkable it is that the features show nothing distinctively Hindu. The hair grows in close crisp curls ; the broad fleshy cheeks might make the face seem heavy, were it not for the marked and dignified expression conferred by the calm forward eyes and acquiline nose, somewhat pointed at the tip. The forehead is of average size, the lips very full and thick, the upper one long almost to ugliness, throwing the chin, though full and prominent, into the shade. The arms which touch the body only at the hips are remarkably long, the large well-formed hands and fingers reaching to the knees ; the exigencies of the posture and material have caused the shoulders where the arms join to be rather disproportionately broad and massive. The feet, each 4 feet and 9 inches long, rest on a stance, wrought from the same

[1] Vol. I., pp. 86.f

rock, that seems small for the immense size and weight (80 tons) of the statue, a lotus stem springing at each foot is carried up in low relief twice round each leg and arm. A brief inscription at the side below tells that the image was erected by king Vīra Pandia in 1432 to Bāhubalin, son of Vishaba, the first Tirthaṅkara of giant race, himself a giant, and therefore so represented, but still in the shape of the founder of that faith whence the Jain heresy diverged. A low cloister runs round the inner side of the enclosing wall, and a massive stone rail of three horizontal bars surrounds the platform. Once in sixty years the scattered Jains gather from all quarters and bathe the colossus with coconut milk."

The curly hair, elongated ears and long arms, were three of the traditional beauty marks of Gautama the Buddha.

Outside the entrance into the walled enclosure containing the statue, is a handsome monolithic *stambha* or pillar surmounted by an image of Brahmā in a sitting posture. The pillar is enclosed by a massive stone railing like those set up by the Buddhists, and is obviously a copy of a wooden structure.

The existing ancient monuments show that Jainism must have been a flourishing religion in Kanara during the middle ages, and their style indicates that they were executed by stone masons from Mysore, who seem to have been the first builders in stone in this part of India. Prior to this period, the religious buildings, palaces and domestic dwellings were of wood, just as they are at the present day on the West Coast. On the decline of Jainism in Kanara and Malabar, stone temple building came to an end, and the people returned to their original wooden style of architecture. Like the hill tribes of the Himalayas, the West Coast people possess excellent carpenters and wood-carvers, but very few stone-masons and sculptors. Again they possess an unlimited supply of fine timber, the timber trade being one of the chief industries of the district. Yet another reason why wood is preferred to stone, is because the local stone is mostly laterite, a very inferior stone for building purposes and quite useless for ornamental structures or sculptural work. Laterite was, and still is, used for the foundations of wooden buildings, and it was also used for memorials to the dead as already mentioned in Chapter I.

As an important religious emblem, the umbrella must have been venerated on the West Coast from very early times and long before the arrival of the Jains from Mysore in the twelfth century A.D., as we find it represented in the earliest rock-cut tombs and memorials to the dead, which were certainly executed long before the advent of the Jains in this part of India. We know from his inscriptions that Asoka sent forth missionaries to Southern India to convert the inhabitants to Buddhism. It is, therefore, possible that it was these early Buddhist missionaries who first introduced the umbrella motif, just as they appear to have done in Ceylon about the same period.

The Jains and Bānts (Hindus) of Kanara, like the Kōṭas of the adjacent Nīlgiris, erect funeral-cars, which are known locally as *dhūpes*, a name which must be a corruption of the Sanskrit word *stūpa*. Originally, these structures were raised over the spot where the remains of a High Priest, or a Chief were cremated, as a temporary memorial, and always in a field or plot of ground specially set apart for the purpose and known as the *bakimar* (the field at the gate), because these fields were usually situated in front of the *gōpuram* or gate-house of a temple, or a Chief's palace. Such fields may be seen in several villages in Kanara, where descendants of some of the old ruling chiefs are still living in their ancestral homes, as at Mūdabidri, the seat of the Chautar Chiefs of South Kanara and the chief centre of Jainism in the district. Here, and in several other places in Kanara, the temporary wooden *dhūpes* were copied in stone as everlasting memorials to the dead. The Mūdabidri group contains about twenty of these quaint monuments all built of laterite stone and standing close together in rows. They are square on plan and vary from 5 to 20 feet in height and are surmounted by granite *kalasas*, most of which are missing. The number of canopies or superimposed roofs of a wooden or stone *dhūpe* varies according to the dignity of the deceased. Generally the High Priests had the largest and tallest *dhūpes* then came the local chiefs. Kanarese inscriptions found on a few of the Mūdabidri *dhūpes* show that they date back to the twelfth century; prior to that date they seem to have been built only of wood. It will be noticed that the corners of the superimposed roofs are decorated with small up-turned granite projections (Fig. 30). The latter represent the simulated ends of wooden rafters, which in the wooden temples of this district always turn upwards at the corners. A similar device, which is supposed to "avert the evil eye", is met with in Nepāl and in the Far East. If any proof were wanting these stone projections alone prove that the masonry built *dhūpe* is merely a stone copy of a wooden one. In other words, it proves that wooden *dhūpes* existed long before the Jain masons thought of building them of laterite.

The Mūdabidri group of *dhūpes* is mentioned and illustrated in Fergusson's *History of Indian and Eastern Architecture* (Vol. II., p. 80), where they are described as Jain tombs. However, they are not tombs, but stone memorials to the dead, marking the spot where the body was cremated, the ashes being thrown into a sacred tank or river ; and they are not peculiar to the Jains, as the Bānts (Hindus) and all the leading land-holding classes of South Kanara follow the custom at the present day, and have done so for centuries. Fergusson never visited the West Coast himself, and his account of the temples of Malabar and South Kanara was written from photographs which he had collected.

The Jains like the Buddhists, believed that their idols and illustrious dead were honoured in direct ratio to the number of canopies or *chhatras* set up over them. A good example of this is shown in Fig. 31, a large and ancient brass model of the Jaina Heaven, or abode of the twenty-four Tirthaṅkaras or Saints. It is designed on similar lines to a wooden funeral-car and is surmounted by a miniature medieval *stūpa* as a finial. Seated in the different storeys are the twenty-four saints, each over-shadowed by a royal umbrella. The four corners of the little *stūpa*-like finial are guarded by lions, as in similar Buddhist monuments. Each cornice is decorated with a simulated fringe like those which adorn the cloth canopies of a funeral-car. Simulated fringes are a common feature of the wooden roofs of the West Coast and Himalayan temples, the fringe is carved on the wooden eaves of the superimposed roofs over the shrine chamber, the roofs resembling in shape and construction the canopies of a baldachin. As an example of this, we may take the picturesque little pavilion belonging to the Kṛishṇa temple at Udipi in South Kanara (Fig. 32). During the Water-festival held at this temple, the image of Kṛishṇa is taken out of the main shrine and set up in the pavilion which stands in the centre of the temple pond. The pavilion thus takes the place of a wooden festival-car. The pillars and base of the structure are of stone, but the double roof is of wood covered with small copper plates. The eaves are decorated with a simulated fringe, and the curved hips of the roofs with serpent heads of copper, while a copper-gilt *kalasa* surmounts the building. This type of double-canopied roof, like the superimposed canopies of a *dhūpe*, is the outcome of the same religious idea of raising honorific *chhatras* over the dead, or above the head of a deity. Double-and triple-canopied wooden roofs of this kind, covered with thatch, tiles or copper plates, some ancient, others modern, are still common on the West Coast, and appear to represent the original and usual style of temple roof before the arrival of the Jain builders from Mysore in the twelfth century.

The religion of the Malayālī is a strange mixture of Animism and Vedantism. The paramount influence of the Brāhmaṇs in all religious and social matters is eveywhere apparent; and yet the West Coast, and Malabar in particular, is pre-eminently the home of witchcraft and magic and all that is indicated by the term Animism. Evidence of a widespread primitive worship of ancestors is to be seen in the rock-cut tombs containing sepulchral urns, described in Chapter I., which are found all over the district; and the cult, which seems in origin to be based on fear of the spirits of the dead and a desire to prevent such unwelcome guests from returning to the abodes of the living, survives in the present death ceremonies which require offerings to be made daily to the deceased in the yard of his house, until his ashes are cast into a river. Similar offerings are also made periodically afterwards, or when domestic calamities and the like indicate that the ghost is getting troublesome and requires propitiation. Animistic, again, is the widespread worship of Badrakālī, the goddess who presides over smallpox and cholera, the worship of trees and serpents, and the common belief in exorcism and witchcraft, in which even Nambūdiri Brāhmaṇs share. On the other hand, the Nambūdiri is the strictest of all Southern Brāhmaṇs in the observances of the precepts of the Vedas. They call themselves Āryans, and not only worship Vedic deities, but devote their lives to keeping up Vedic ritual, and their legendary transmigration to Malabar from Northern India is doubtless correct.

Typical of the two elements in the Malayālī's religion are the two classes into which his shrines can be roughly divided. First there are the *ambalams*, which are temples dedicated to the leading deities of the Hindu pantheon, Siva and Vishṇu, and their consorts and incarnations; and secondly the *Kāvus*, smaller shrines, at which the inferior deities such as Subrahmaṇya, Gaṇesa, Ayyappan, Badrakālī, the goddess of smallpox, and malignant demons, such as Kuttichāttan, Mundian and Gulikhan, are propitiated with sacrifice, while their wishes are interpreted by oracles.

In style and construction, the West Coast temples, like the houses, are totally different from those of the East Coast. The central shrine, or *srīkovil*, containing the *liṅga* or image, is usually a small rectangular cell enclosed by a narrow circumambulatory passage surmounted by a double-canopied wooden roof covered with thatch, copper plates, or tiles.

Thatch was probably the first material used for covering these wooden roofs, but the use of copper for this purpose goes back to very early times. In shape and size, the small copper sheets are like tiles and arranged in a similar manner. Owing to the number of important tile works in Malabar, tiles are generally used in these days whenever a new temple is built or an old one repaired. Formerly, under Native rule tiled roofs were a prerogative (jealously guarded) of temples and of Nambūdiris. It was as a special favour that permission was granted to the early English merchants at Calicut by the Zamorin to tile their factory. The construction of a *gōpuram* or gate-house also could not be undertaken without the sanction of the local chieftain, and even at the present day the anger of some village tyrant may be aroused by the usurpation of such privileges without permission.

The *srīkovil*, or main shrine, stands on a raised plaftorm built of stone. The walls of the shrine chamber and circumambulatory passage, which in all the larger temples always surrounds the sanctum, are usually of masonry, but when of timber construction, the spaces between the timber-framed walls are screened by a curious kind of horizontal lattice-work peculiar to the West Coast, and constructed on similar lines to the wooden railings of the Buddhists. The heavy double-canopied wooden roof with widely projecting eaves is supported from below by carved wooden struts, similar to those found in the temples of Nepāl. The *srīkovil* stands inside a quadrangle, enclosed by a low verandah with a tiled roof which runs all round the enclosure. The latter usually contains a few minor shrines, rooms for cooking and feeding (*agrasālās*) and a well. The main entrance into the quadrangle generally faces the east, and consists of a porch surmounted by an ornamental gable of wooden construction decorated with a carved bargeboard, pendants and finials. This ornamental gable is one of the chief characteristics of West Coast architecture. The apex of the gable is usually decorated with a carved wooden head of a demon with protruding tongue and serpent canopy, while the ends of the bargeboard are provided with wooden arms and hands, which gives the bargeboard the appearance of two long arms pointing downwards, suggesting a demon protecting the entrance from evil spirits. The bargeboard of the gable is often decorated with a fringe and supported by small wooden pillars. The back of the gable is of wood and is usually carved and painted in gay colours. The interior of the porch is provided with a coffered wooden ceiling ornamented with carved bas-relief figures of Hindu deities, religious symbols and floral patterns, also gaily painted. Standing in front of the porch of the more important temples, may be seen a tall wooden flagstaff covered with brass, and close to it, a stone or metal lamp-pillar (*dīpastambha*), usually the gift of some wealthy patron of the temple.

The larger temples have an outer walled enclosure with a gateway facing the public road. This enclosure seems to have been provided mainly for the benefit of the lower castes, who are not permitted to enter the inner quadrangle of the temple.

The officiating priests in the larger temples are Nambūdiris and only Brāhmaṇs are permitted to enter the *srīkovil*, while low-caste people may not go beyond the *pīpal*, or Bodhi-tree, in the outer enclosure. At festival times a small image of the deity is placed near the tree with a collection-box into which the votaries of the polluting castes drop their cash or jewel offerings.

Congregational worship not being a feature of Hinduism, the daily services of washing the idol, offering food, &c., are conducted by the priest within closed doors to the music of drums, pipes and cymbals. The ordinary worshipper comes with his offerings (flowers, food, money or jewels, which are given to the priest), enters the quadrangle, stands in front of the shrine, bows with joined palms and mutters a prayer which is usually the simple expression of a request made in the colloquial vernacular and is not couched in set phrases. The educated few recite Sanskrit verses praising the deity. Having made this prayer, the worshipper performs *pradakshinam*, that is, he walks round the quadrangle keeping the shrine on his right hand, once, twice, seven times or more, according to the fervour of his devotion; makes another bow before the shrine muttering his prayer; receives *prasādam* (flowers and sandal powder, &c., which have been offered to the idol) from the priest, and departs.

The Nambūdiris are Vedic Brāhmaṇs and in the main worshippers of Siva, but throughout Malabar there is little sectarianism and no strict differentiation between the worship of Siva and Vishṇu. They perform the *Sandhyāvandhanam* or daily worship of the sun, and observe the chief Vedic festivals and fasts (*vratams*). They do not, as a rule, worship any but Purāṇic gods, but they occasionally make offerings at serpent shrines; and they recognize the existence of evil spirits, whom they exorcise by means of special *mantrams*. The *pīpal* tree, the Brāhmaṇī kite, and the *tulasī* plant, or basil, are sacred in their eyes. High caste Nāyars follow most of the religious practices of the Nambūdiris, but they are not permitted to read the Vedas or perform Vedic rites; and tree, serpent, and ancestor worship occupy a more important place in their religion. The lower classes of Sūdras pay less attention to the Purāṇic gods, and worship in temples is confined in their case to festive occasions. They assign most of the troubles of this life to the witchcraft of enemies, to the malignity of demons or ghosts of the departed, or to the evil eye. On the occurrence of any disease or calamity, they consult the local astrologer, who divines the evil spirit responsible and names the exorcist who can best deal with the case, and prescribes the mode of worship best suited to the occasion. The deities most worshipped are Subrahmanya, Gaṇesa Badrakālī, and Kuttichāttan, the most terrible of the demons. The Malayālī is exceedingly superstitious, and it is remarkable how large a number of people in Malabar make their living by exorcism and magic.

The *kāvu* or *bhūtasthānam* is usually an unpretentious little structure, mainly of wood, with the characteristic tiled roof with widely projecting eaves, while the more important shrines have a double roof of the usual kind. The deities are the sons of Siva, the incarnations of his consort, or the innumerable host of his *bhūtas* or demons.

Ancestors are worshipped sometimes in special *kāvus*, or in small outhouses or special rooms in the house. Generally there is no daily worship, but there are periodical commemorations on the anniversary of the ancestor's death, or whenever the ghost proves troublesome.

Serpent shrines, known as *nāgattan-kāvu*, are to be found in the gardens of most of the private houses, and their worship occupies a prominent place in the religious life of the Nāyars. The *kāvu* consists of a clump of jungle trees festooned with creepers, the whole being sacred and scrupulously reserved; in the middle are often small snake-stones (*nāga-kals*), the gifts of women who have been blessed with children. The serpent is regarded as the tutelary deity of the house, and god and shrine are conveyed with property and frequently specified in deeds of transfer. Worship is offered at least once a year, often by a Brāhmaṇ; and the serpents propitiated by songs and dances called *nāgapāttu*, which are supposed to be effective in procuring offspring. The high priest of the serpent cult in Malabar is the Pamban-Mākkād Nambūdiri, who lives at Ponnāni in a house full of cobras, which are said to be harmless to him and his family.

Beypore is a small but ancient seaport at the mouth of the Beypore river which flows into the sea a few miles south of Calicut. The little town contains a fine old Siva temple called the Mahādeva Kovil, which is a good example of early West Coast architecture, but alas, is rapidly falling into decay through neglect and lack of funds (Figs. 33 and 34).

The temple contains a *liṅga* as the object of worship, and faces the west. It stands on a raised granite basement about 3 feet high, with a flight of steps leading up to the entrance. The stone-work is nicely carved. Above the rounded moulding of the plinth is a row of rectangular stone projections running all round the plinth, in much the same manner as modillions decorate a Greek cornice. These projections simulate the heads of wooden floor joists, and indicate that the builders were ordinarily accustomed to timber construction. The basement of the Beypore temple is of solid stone and the floor paved with granite slabs, but in the wooden temples of the West Coast and Himalayas, the floors are often of wood, consisting of planks nailed to joists which rest on stone foundations, the heads of the joists projecting a few inches outwards along the plinth line, in the same manner as they are simulated here in stone (Fig. 34). This helps to prove that wooden temples are far older than stone-built structures, and, in fact, that the latter are mainly stone models of former wooden buildings.

The temple consists of a square sanctum surrounded by two circum-ambulatory passages, an unusual feature, though most early Hindu temples of importance are provided with one passage for this purpose. On each side of the entrance is a large four-armed figure of a door-keeper armed with a huge club. The style of these figures indicates the twelfth century as the probable date of the temple. The two roofs are of wood and the walls of the shrine chamber of stone. The widely projecting eaves are supported from below by carved struts similar to those found in Himalayan temples. The massive and elaborate construction of these wooden roofs is shown in Fig. 35. The main beam on which the rafters rest is ornamented underneath with a row of painted wooden pendants, suggesting simulated tassels.

Both roofs are covered with tiles of an ancient pattern—leaf-shaped, which gives them a pleasing appearance. Owing to the numerous modern tile works which have sprung up on the West Coast, these ancient tiles are rare in these days and will soon be a thing of the past. The hips of the roof are protected by broad bands of white mortar and turn up at the corners. This concave form of the roof is produced by small serpentine wooden brackets fixed to the heads of the angle rafters, partly to keep the mortar above from slipping down, but mainly to serve as a safeguard against maglignant spirits (Fig. 33). When the roofs are covered with copper, these serpent brackets are also made of that metal as may be seen in Fig. 32.

The walls of the wooden gallery above the sanctum are decorated with wood-carving and in the centre of each wall is a niche containing an ancient wooden image of the following Hindu deities—Siva on the south wall, Vishṇu on the north, Brahmā on the east and Narasinha (the Man-lion incarnation of Vishṇu) on the west. Since the temple is dedicated to Siva and contains a *liṅga* as the object of worship, this collection of Hindu deities in the gallery above the shrine chamber appears to represent the abode of the leading gods of the Hindu pantheon, who in this case, watch over Mahādeva in the sanctum below. Like the temples in Nepāl, the wooden struts supporting the roof of the gallery are carved in the form of *yālis* (leogryphs) as safeguards against evil spirits. A copper-gilt *kalasa* originally crowned the top of the temple but is now missing.

The Malayālī maiden shown in the foreground of Fig. 34 belongs to the Vāriyar caste whose traditional duty is to sweep the temple precincts (*vāruga*). Like many other castes on the West Coast, the women, like the men, wear only a waist cloth. This is a very ancient custom that is portrayed in the earliest Buddhist sculptures and seems to have been universal in India in early times.

CHAPTER IV.

Himalayan Architecture.

Although the wooden temples of the Himalayas, from Kashmīr to Nepāl, are comparatively modern structures, they illustrate better than any other examples the extraordinary influence which the umbrella motif had on the development of Indian architecture, and, at the same time, explain how the many-roofed wooden pagodas of China and Japan originated. As representative of this class of monuments, we may take the wooden temples of Kulū where every village has its own little wooden shrine.

Kulū is a subdivision of the Kāngra district of the Panjāb and comprises the Upper Biās Valley, Waziri Rūpi, Sarāj, Lāhul and Spiti. On the north it is bounded by Ladākh, on the east by Tibet, on the west by the principalities of Chambā, Mandī and Sukēt, on the south by the Sutlej and the Bashahr States. For administrative purposes this tract is now divided into two regions, called Kulū and Sarāj.

The ancient name of the district was Kulūta when Hiuen Tsang visited the country in the beginning of the seventh century A.D., and in those days it formed a separate state. He makes mention of a "Buddha's *stūpa*, built by Asoka in the middle of the country to commemorate the Buddha's visit to the district". He further tells us that in his time there were twenty monasteries and about a thousand Buddhist priests. There were also fifteen Hindu temples, which different sects used without distinction. This shows how flourishing Buddhism must have been in Kulū in the seventh century, though it has now practically disappeared, the existing religion being a curious mixture of Lamaism and Hinduism.

Though most of the hill tribes profess the Hindu religion, local goddesses of the Durgā or Kālī type, combined with the worship of trees, serpents and demons, appeal to these simple hill folk to a far greater extent than the recognized deities of the Hindu pantheon. And in this respect, their religion is strikingly similar to that prevailing among the Hindus of the West Coast. Their picturesque wooden shrines are rectangular on plan and usually provided with an open, or closed circumambulatory passage around the sanctum, a feature also common to the temples of Malabar. The temples are built almost entirely of wood, only the substructures and spaces between the timber-framed walls being of masonry with horizontal layers of roughly hewn logs. The wooden pillars supporting the widely projecting eaves and the doors and windows are often richly carved with floral patterns, birds, serpents, demons and Hindu deities. The front of the temple is provided with an ornamental gable above the entrance with carved bargeboards ornamented with a hanging wooden fringe, while a heavy ridge-beam decorated with wooden or metal finials surmounts the roof which is covered with shingles or roughly hewn slates. The shrines are usually picturesquely situated in a forest glade on the outskirts of the village. They are of all sizes and ages; while some are quite modern, others are really ancient structures, as we know from inscriptions found in them. The smaller shrines have a plain gable roof, but the more important temples have double- or triple-canopied wooden roofs, placed one above the other like those of the West Coast temples. Temples in this style are typical of Himalayan architecture and are best known from Kashmīr to Nepāl. The three best examples in Kulū are—the Hiḍimbā temple at Manāli, a village in the upper Biās valley, that of Tripurasundarī Devī at Nagar, the ancient capital of Kulū, and the Triyuga Nārāyaṇa temple at Dyār on the left bank of the Biās, opposite the town of Bajūra.

The great event in the lives of the people of Kulū, is the annual fair and great *Doum* festival held in the summer at Sultānpur, the modern capital. At this season all the people of the surrounding villages gather at Sultānpur bringing with them their local deities in procession. These idols are usually small metal masks of the goddess Durgā in some form or other. In most of the village shrines may be seen a number of brass and silver masks of this kind presented by worshippers in place of cash or ordinary jewels. They are known as *doums*, and are made out of a thin sheet of embossed silver or brass about 9 inches square, representing the head of the deity only. The features are often well modelled and the eyes sometimes set with precious stones, while some of them are inscribed. One temple in Kulū possesses a set of gold masks presented by Rājā Bahādur Singh, who was the ruler of Kulū in the sixteenth century. During the great car-festivals held in the plains, the stone images enshrined within the temples are not carried in procession, their place being taken by smaller duplicate images made of metal. And so it is that in the Himalayan districts the stone images remain in their shrines, and only the *doums* and other jewels are taken to the festival. Owing to the nature of the country, the use of festival-cars with wheels is impossible, so the *doums* are carried in procession on a light wooden structure known as a *ratha*, which when draped with a coloured cloth and surmounted by a couple of superimposed umbrellas becomes a portable shrine (Fig. 36). The lower portion consists of a light wooden frame built round a single staff which supports the canopies of the umbrellas. The construction of the *ratha* is similar to that of the Kōta funeral-car in the Nīlgiris (Fig. 5) ; it also bears a remarkable resemblance to the Buddha's funeral-car illustrated in Fig. 4. When covered with a cloth canopy, the lower portion of the *ratha* represents the shrine chamber, while the superimposed umbrellas simulate the two roofs of a Himalayan temple. In the example shown here, the big lower umbrella is of wood with an ornamental brass band round the edge and is covered with black yaks' tails and a yellow cloth. Surmounting the latter, is a small umbrella of brass with a hanging fringe of the same metal. Similar metal umbrellas may be seen in some of the temples in Southern India.

When taken in procession, the *ratha* is fixed on two long staves and carried like a sedan-chair by two priests or other men belonging to the temple, the one in front walking backwards so as to avoid turning his back on the deity. Thus borne, and escorted by all the leading people of the village, dancing and singing before the *ratha* to the wild music of pipes, drums and cymbals, is the *rathyātrā* or car-festival performed in the Himalayas ; and a wonderfully picturesque sight it is to watch the gay procession wending its way through the primeval forest, over hill and dale, until at last the temple is reached, in front of which the *ratha* is set down and a priest washes the masks of the goddess with wild mint leaves and water, and then offers incence, flowers and fruit. A goat is sacrificed and the blood collected in a brass bowl and offered to the goddess, and a feast brings the ceremony to a close.

According to Hiuen Tsang, Buddhists were settled in Kulū as early as 250 B.C. or thereabouts, and by 650 A.D. there were over twenty monasteries and hundreds of Buddhist priests. We know that they used *rathas* at their funerals and festivals, so perhaps they introduced the car-festival into Kulū. Whether the *ratha* is derived from a wooden temple of the Himalayan type, or whether the latter is merely a permanent model of the *ratha*, is a moot point ; but this much is certain, that both religious structures are intimately connected and are the outcome of the same intense veneration for the umbrella motif which prevailed in India in early times.

If we compare the roof of a typical Himalayan temple with the *ratha* shown in Fig. 36, the connection between the two is obvious. For this purpose we may take the roof of the old Siva temple at Kumhārsen, a village in the Simla district which adjoins Kulū (Fig. 37). The umbrella roof of this temple, including the hanging fringe is entirely of wood and is crowned by a copper finial. Its interior construction is similar to that of a state umbrella, only on stronger lines to support the heavy wooden canopy. Its conical shape is mainly due to the nature of the material out of which it is built, but large ceremonial umbrellas of this shape, covered with yellow silk and adorned with a fringe, are still met with in Burma and Siam, and in all probability were common in India in the palmy days of Buddhism.

Below the umbrella canopy of the Kumhārsen temple is a second roof in the form of a rectangular canopy with projecting eaves ornamented with a fringe and covered with slates. It is clear that these two upper roofs are purely ornamental and honorific like the superimposed canopies of a *ratha,* which they closely resemble. It would have been far easier and cheaper to have had a straight-lined roof with a gable at each end. The extraordinary manner in which the eaves of the lower, or main roof, are projected outwards and curve upwards, together with the fringe decorating the eaves-board, suggests that this roof simulates the canopy of a cloth-covered baldachin. The presence of the fringe alone indicates this, as it is difficult to imagine a more unsuitable architectural ornament for a wooden or stone building than a simulated silk fringe.

In the picturesque village of Dalas in Kulū, is another old Siva temple similar to the one at Kumhārsen. It is known as the Jogeshar Mahādeo temple and is built entirely of deodar wood, including its floor, which is covered with planks nailed to wooden joists resting on stone foundations (Fig. 38). As is usual in such structures, the ends of the floor joists protrude outwards along the plinth line of the building. If we compare the wooden plinth of the Dalas temple with the stone one of the Beypore temple (Fig. 34), the meaning and origin of the row of small rectangular stone projections decorating the base of the Beypore temple becomes manifest at once. It also helps to prove that the stone temples are derived from wooden prototypes.

The Dalas temple consists of the usual square sanctum enclosed by a narrow processional passage with a pillared porch in front surmounted by an ornamental gable. The three roofs are similar to those of the Kumhārsen temple. The uppermost roof is covered with wooden shingles, and the two lower ones with slates. Originally, the eaves of all three roofs were ornamented with the usual wooden fringe. The angles of the middle roof are decorated with little metal bells, a common feature of Himalayan temples, intended to scare away evil spirits, while the ridge-beam surmounting the roof is ornamented with small copper *kalasas* and iron tridents. The pillars in the porch, the wooden railing round the latter and the shrine doorway are nicely carved.

The next step in the development of the Himalayan temple is well represented by the Temple of Triyuga Nārāyaṇa (Vishṇu) at Dyār in Kulū (Fig. 39). Here we find the three superimposed roofs assuming the form of a storeyed wooden tower above the sanctum. The two lower roofs are built in the usual style, while the upper one unmistakably represents a large wooden umbrella surmounted by a tall wooden finial decorated with a miniature metal umbrella. The temple is square on plan and contains an image of Vishṇu. The two upper floors are blind storeys and serve no useful purpose. This is so in all temples built in this style, not only in India but also in China and Japan. The construction and ornamentation of the building is similar to that of the Dalas temple, except that the walls of the ground floor are of rubble masonry alternated with layers of wood to bind the courses together. The lower roofs are covered with slates and the upper one with shingles. The building in front represents a later addition and is not an integral part of the original structure. It will be noticed that the two storeys are marked by a well defined cornice decorated with a wooden fringe, while bells were originally suspended from the angles of the roof.

On proceeding up the Kulū Valley from Dyār in a northerly direction, along the old caravan route to Ladākh, one comes to the village of Maṇālī, situated on the right bank of the Biās, and about a hundred miles north of Simla. On the outskirts of the village, almost hidden by giant deodars, stands the picturesque wooden temple of the goddess Hiḍimbā, a man-eating *rākshasī* or demoness, to whom human sacrifices used to be made within the living memory of the local people. An inscription carved on the left jamb of the wooden doorway records that the temple was built by Rājā Bahādur Singh in 1553 A.D. (Fig. 40). In this example we find the number of roofs surmounting the shrine increased to four. The three lower ones are in the usual form of projecting canopies, showing traces of the wooden fringe here and there. A large wooden umbrella, surmounted by a metal finial, crowns the summit of the temple and thus forms the fourth roof. All the roofs are of wood and covered with shingles. The shrine doorway and the windows on each side of it are richly carved and present a handsome appearance, while over the entrance is a wooden balcony. It is one of the oldest wooden temples in Kulū, but this does not imply that its architectural style is therefore earlier than that of the last three examples. On the contrary, its style indicates that it is a development of the Dyār type of temple, which on plan and in construction it closely resembles. An inscription on a building is useful in fixing the date of the structure, but as a rule it throws no light on the antiquity of the style of the building. The latter depends on many things, but mainly on the progressive skill attained by the local builders and the amount of support received from wealthy patrons. Thus, in some remote village where there was a lack of both skill and patronage, the local builders would continue to build primitive little gable-roofed shrines like those erected by their ancestors of a bygone period. Therefore, in tracing the origin and development of any particular style of architecture, one must not rely on inscriptions alone.

Hiḍimbā is, or certainly was, the patron saint of Kulū, and in all probability, a primitive wooden shrine dedicated to her existed at Manālī long before Bahādur Singh built the present temple. The Rājā was naturally anxious that his temple should surpass all others in size and splendour, and he was able to command the services of the best carpenters and woodcarvers in the district to ensure this. Being an important temple, its roofs have doubtless been repaired from time to time since it was first built, thus accounting for its good state of preservation.

The temples of Nepāl are of a more advanced type than those of Kulū, and represent the last stage in the development of this style of Indian architecture. The striking resemblance between the temples of Nepāl and those of China and Japan, indicates that it was mainly through Nepāl, *via* Tibet and Korea, that this ancient style of wooden architecture found its way into those countries.

I am personally familiar with the temples of Kulū and Sarāj, but I have not visited Nepāl, so must rely on the works of others in giving a brief description of the Nepālese temples here. For this purpose I cannot do better than quote from Mr. Percy Brown's fascinating book —*Picturesque Nepāl*, as this work is well illustrated and contains excellent descriptions of the arts and architecture of the State. A description of the chief monuments in Nepāl will also be found in Volume I. of Fergusson's *History of Indian and Eastern Architecture*, but the illustrations are poor, and Fergusson never visited Nepāl himself. For some unknown reason, the Archæological Survey of India has never made a survey of the ancient monuments in Nepāl, and yet it is here, above all other parts of the country where one might reasonably expect to find many of the missing links in the history of Indian architecture. Nepāl, like Kulū, was never seriously affected by the wave of Islām which swept the Peninsula from end to end in the twelfth and following centuries. The storm, raging in the plains of India, was spent before it reached the natural ramparts of Nepāl, and for this reason, the country is of exceptional interest, as it illustrates to a considerable extent the state of India before Islām had imprinted its mark on most aspects of the life of the country. The manners and customs, the religion and the art and architecture of the inhabitants of Nepāl, are much the same to-day as they were ten centuries ago, and thus the State preserves an ideal picture of India in the Middle Ages. Before attempting to describe the Nepālese temples, it is necessary to say something about the people and history of this little known country. It seems that the original inhabitants are the Nevārs, while the present ruling race are the Gurkhas, who conquered the country as recently as 1768. The Nevārs are said to have originally come from Tibet and its vicinity, and settled in Nepāl in remote times. They now form the bulk of the population of the ancient capitals of Pāṭan and Bhāṭgāon. As carpenters, woodcarvers and metalworkers, they are clever and skilful, and the picturesque appearance of old Nepāl is mainly due to the artistic temperament of the Nevārs. The woodcarving and embossed metal work on the sacred buildings and palaces is one of the most characteristic features of the State. As in other parts of India, this art is connected almost entirely with the religion of the people, and to understand it, some reference to the cult of those responsible for its production is necessary.

The prevailing religion of the Nevārs is Buddhism, and has been so ever since 250 B.C., when Asoka visited Nepāl and made Buddhism the religion of the State. In commemoration of his visit, Asoka is credited with having built five *stūpas*, one in the centre of Pāṭan, and the others at the four cardinal points round the city. What particular dynasty held sway at the time of Asoka's visit is not clear, and we do not come to historical fact until the fifth century A.D., when we meet with the earliest inscriptions.[1] They belong to the later kings of the Lichchhavi dynasty, whose ancestors came from Vaisālī and established themselves in Nepāl, and appear to have been mainly followers of Siva. Buddhism however, seems to have still remained the chief religion

[1] *Indian Antiquary*, Vol. IX., pp. 163–194.

of the country, but the ruling race were Hindus, who endeavoured to introduce into the temples the cult of Siva. In this manner were the two religions brought into contact, a state in which they exist at the present day. The Lichchhavi inscriptions range from the latter part of the fifth century to the seventh, when Aṁsuvarman founded a new dynasty known as the Thākurī. In 1097, Nānyadeva of Tirhūt invaded and subjugated the country, and again in 1324 Harisiṁha of the same race assumed the Government. But this dynasty does not appear to have ruled for long, and the four chief towns—Bhāṭgāon, Banepa, Pāṭan, and Kāṭhmaṇḍū had each their own princes till the year 1768, when a weak ruler having called in the assistance of a neighbouring Gurkha Rājā, the latter seized the kingdom for himself, and his successors still rule in Nepāl.

The high standard of the doctrine and discipline that marked the character of early Buddhism has become considerably modified in Nepāl by the introduction of many of the more popular features of modern Hinduism, and thus the religion has lost much of the chaste and simple character for which it was originally noted. In this manner, we find in the precincts of a Nepālese temple, a medley of Hindu and Buddhist symbols and images. A temple in Nepāl will often display an image of the Buddha, calm, dignified and reposeful, while in close proximity is placed a many-armed figure of Kālī, symbolizing all that is restless and terrible in a faith which rules by fear. Interwoven with these two creeds is a third form of worship. Peering from under the broad eaves of the temples in the form of woodcarving, or leering in gaudy colours from the red walls of the temples, the Tantric element of Nepālese Buddhism appears in many architectural forms. Who and what are the devotees of this unhallowed cult is never divulged, but that it has a firm hold on a large community is proved by the frequency with which its various aspects are pictorially expressed.

Concerning the woodcarving adorning these temples, Mr. Brown says :—" Of what may be termed the minor arts of Nepāl, that of the worker in wood is the most important, and in his productions this craftsman has been even more prolific than the metalworker. But he has rarely if ever aspired to statuary in this material, although his caryatid [roof] struts are at times such wonderful figure groups that they may almost be classed as fine art. But regarded broadly, the Nevār woodworker has subordinated his handiwork and utilized it mainly in conjunction with the architect, so that his conceptions come within the category of the applied arts. In his carved tympanums those large characteristic panels applied over all Nepālī doorways—the woodworker has been allowed considerable latitude, and these features are often complete pictures, religious subjects sculptured out of wood, and treated with a freedom which adds not a little to their charm. The motive of these 'over-doors', whether in wood or metal, is ordinarily the same general idea—a story in the centre depicting a mythological incident, or a pictorial arrangement of various deities, while around the whole in high relief is displayed a kind of traditional convention of Garuḍa, Makara, Nāgas, and ornament, nearly always composed on the same general lines. A picturesque detail, and one on which the Nevār woodcarver delighted to show his skill and versatility, is the aforementioned roof-strut, supporting the wide overhanging eaves of the pagodas. The broad roofs of these buildings naturally throw deep shadows, and the duty of breaking up this dark mass with some light and graceful design was left to the artistic devices of this craftsman. This individual conceived the idea of converting these constructive elements into figures of deities provided with many arms, and the problem was solved in a most satisfactory manner. The light catches on these fanciful figures with their outspread arms, and the heavy appearance of this shadow is at once corrected, and an artistic and picturesque effect attained. But this is only one of the many clever contrivances invented by the Nevār woodworker to overcome constructive difficulties of a like nature. That useful element in sound building, the wooden lintel, is a special characteristic of Nepālese architecture, and the decorative treatment of this forms an important feature of the style. A masonry composed of a good red brick flashed with a kind of half glaze, and bound with beams of *sāl* timber, is the manner in which the builder carried out his work in the days of the Nevār kings, and over this sensible solid framework the metal and wood worker were allowed to bring their artistic fancies into play, with a result in every sense satisfying. This structural device of the lintel, as used in connection with the doors and windows, gives the buildings of Nepāl their distinctive character, and the particular beam above and below the window, treated in the Nevār manner, is the keynote of the whole design. Foliated and elaborated, moulded and corbelled, this constructive element was the joy of the woodcarver, who brought all his artistic energies to bear on its embellishment. The consequence is that the window, in Nepālese buildings, has rarely received more ornate treatment in the history of art ".[1]

[1] *Picturesque Napāl*, pp. 169–172.

On plan and in design, the Nepālese temple is similar to those found in the Himalayan districts further west. The plan is square, and the ground floor is the only part of the structure put to any practical use, the upper floors, which may be several in number, being blind storeys which are purely ornamental and honorific. The chamber on the ground floor stands on a raised masonry plinth with a flight of steps leading up to the entrance. The sanctum is plain and contains nothing but the object of worship and a few religious accessories. But outside, the doors and windows are usually lavishly decorated with superb woodcarving and embossed metal work. The walls are of a good red brick, and the superimposed wooden roofs with their widely projecting eaves, are covered with tiles or copper plates. The angles of the roof canopies turn upwards like those of the West Coast temples which they closely resemble. The eaves are supported from below by a row of carved wooden struts, as in Malabar. The eaves are ornamented with both wooden and metal fringes, the latter often in the form of a row of small metal bells, a very ancient device which first appears carved on the coping of the stone railing of the Bharhut Stūpa (*circa* 180 B.C.). The tongues of these little bells are small leaf-shaped brass pendants similar to those which form the fringe of the metal umbrella which surmounts the Himalayan *ratha* shown in Fig. 36.

In Fig. 41, we have two typical Nepālese temples which are situated in the old Darbar square of the ancient capital of Pāṭan. The one in the centre is the temple of Bhairab; that on the left is dedicated to Kṛishṇa, and has two large stone elephants guarding the entrance which is approached by a flight of stone steps. None of the Nepālese temples appear much earlier than the sixteenth century, so we do not know what the earliest wooden examples were like, but it is reasonable to suppose they were similar to those of Kulū, since the existing temples retain so many features common to both styles. The Nevārs being a far more artistic race than the inhabitants of the Western Himalayas, would naturally improve on the original style and develop it on their own lines, and with most satisfactory results, but at the same time there is good reason to believe that in the seventh century A.D., and long before that, there existed in India plenty of wooden temples and monasteries which were in no way inferior to the existing ones in Nepāl; in fact some of them, according to the descriptions left us by the Chinese pilgrims cited above, even surpassed the Nepālese temples in size and splendour. There is Sung Yun's account of the *Tsioh-li* pagoda at Peshāwar built by King Kanishka (*circa* 100 A.D.), a carved wooden structure of thirteen storeys already mentioned in Chapter II. Then we have Fa Hian's account of the famous Jētavana monastery at Srāvastī, which, he says, originally had seven storeys. "The kings of the surrounding countries and the people vied with each other in making religious offerings at the spot. They decked the structure with flags and silken canopies (umbrellas); they offered flowers and incense, whilst the lamps shone out all night long. A rat gnawing at the wick of one of the lamps caused it to set fire to one of the canopies, resulting in a general conflagration and the entire destruction of the seven storeys of the building." This account clearly indicates that the storeys were of wooden construction. Fa Hian tells us that the monastery contained a central shrine in which was an ancient sandalwood image of the Buddha in a sitting posture, and that this image escaped destruction by fire. This was probably owing to the walls of the shrine chamber being of brick as was usually the case then and now. He states that this wooden image of the Buddha was the first ever made, and that all subsequent ages followed this model. Wooden images, like wooden temples, existed long before stone ones, and there is no doubt that this sandalwood image was a very ancient one, and belonging as it did to one of the oldest and most important Buddhist monasteries in India, it would naturally be repeatedly copied in later times as the oldest and most orthodox portrait figure of the Buddha, and would thus help to fix the conventional type of image which from about 500 A.D. onwards became universal, being adopted in every country where Buddhism took root. We are told that when Hiuen Tsang returned to China in 645 A.D., he not only brought back a lot of Buddhist books and manuscripts, but also six images of the Buddha. Of these, two were of gold, one of silver, and three of sandalwood. It is probable that at least one of the sandalwood images was a copy of the Jētavana figure, and no doubt served as a model in China in the seventh and subsequent centuries.

Again there is Hiuen Tsang's description of the *Ti-lo-shi-ka* monastery in the ancient kingdom of Magadha, the three main shrines of which seem to have been similar to the existing Nepālese temples. He says that in the road facing the middle gate there were three *vihāras*, above each of which was a (metal) *chhatrāvali*, from which bells were suspended, below they were constructed storey above storey, from the bottom to the top. The storeys were surrounded by railings, and the doors, windows, pillars, beams and staircases were all carved [and covered] with gilt-copper in relief, the intervals being highly decorated. The central

8——J. N. 55882 (6/36)

vihāra contained a standing wooden image of the Buddha 30 feet high, the one on the left an image of Tārā, and that on the right a figure of Avalokitesvara, the two last being of stone. The word *vihāra* really means a monastery, but as every *vihāra* of any importance contained a temple enshrining an image of the Buddha, the Chinese pilgrims use the word to denote both kinds of buildings, especially storeyed wooden structures.

I have mentioned in Chapter II. how Hwei-Sang, a brother pilgrim who accompanied Sung-Yun to Peshāwar, was so impressed by the beauty of King Kanishka's wooden storeyed pagoda that he employed an artist to depict it on copper, and this engraving was doubtless taken back to China. The Chinese records relate that in 652 A.D., after Hiuen Tsang's return to China, he built a pagoda (*Feou-to*) to contain the sacred books and images which he had collected in India. "The total height of this pagoda was 180 feet, and it was built after the model of the Indian pagodas and had five storeys" (*See* Beal's *Life of Hiuen Tsang*, p. 216). There is thus plenty of evidence to show that the first Buddhist monuments erected in the Far East were models of Indian buildings of the sixth and seventh centuries. Buddhist books began to be imported into China as early as 200 A.D., and the Chinese pilgrims whose names are cited above were not the only converts to visit India, but the fact remains, that prior to Hiuen Tsang's return to China in 645 A.D., Buddhist art and architecture does not appear to have had much influence in that country. It was not until Buddhism had become the prevailing, or fashionable, religion of China that any Buddhist buildings were required in that country. Prior to that period there was no demand for such buildings, and when the demand did come and having no other precedent to guide them, the Chinese builders were compelled to construct their pagodas on similar lines to the Buddhist temples of India of that period, which explains why the earliest pagodas of China and Japan bear such a striking resemblance to existing examples in India. In later times, the Chinese and Japanese developed this Indian style of wooden architecture on their own lines, until at last, they evolved a style of religious architecture of their own, which to-day we speak of as Chinese or Japanese, as the case may be, and which most people imagine originated in the Far East.

Prior to the sixth century A.D., Japan was a comparatively uncivilized country and the religion of the people was a primitive cult of the dead. But in the seventh century, at the instigation of Prince Shotoku, Buddhist priests, builders and scholars arrived from Korea; Nara became the capital, and in a few years the Koreans founded the famous Buddhist monastery of Horiuji, an historical event which marks the birth of Japan as a civilized power.

The Horiuji monastery is a very large one and forms a good example of a medieval Buddhist monastery, because the style of the original work seems to have been carefully retained in all subsequent rebuilding. Although the subordinate buildings are comparatively modern, they are in all probability perfectly reliable models of early Korean work. The earliest and most important structures in the group consist of a fine two-storeyed gate-house or *gōpuram*, similar in style and construction to some still existing in Malabar, an oblong two-storeyed temple, and a four-storeyed wooden pagoda resembling a Nepālese temple. These three buildings form but a small part of the great monastery of Horiuji, but they are the only ones which unquestionably date back to the seventh century A.D. As in the Himalayan examples, these early Japanese Buddhist temples are built on a raised basement of brick or stone, with a flight of steps leading up to the entrance of the shrine. They are square on plan, and the walls of the shrine chamber are of brick or stone. As in the Himalayan temples, the ground floor alone is put to any practical use, the superimposed wooden storeys being purely honorific. Running through the Horiuji pagoda, from the stone-paved floor to finial, is an immense wooden staff 100 feet high, 3 feet in thickness at the bottom and 9 inches at the top. The five superimposed wooden roofs of this shrine, which are covered with tiles and curve upwards at the angles, like those of the Malabar and Himalayan temples, are built round this central wooden staff in exactly the same manner as the canopies of a Kōta funeral-car. The base of this staff is provided with a tenon which fits into a hole cut in the centre of the stone floor so as to keep the staff in position. To the top of the pole is fixed a tall metal *chhatrāvali*, similar to those which were common in India at the time when the Horiuji temple was built by carpenters from Korea in the seventh century A.D.

Close to the old Buddhist town of Nara, stands the Yākushiji temple, built in 680 A.D. It is similar in style and construction to the Horiuji pagoda, but here we find the projecting roof canopies supported by struts and wooden pillars with corbel-capitals as in the Indian wooden temples of the same period. The Yākushiji temple is surmounted by a tall iron *chhatrāvali* ornamented with nine gilt-copper *chhatras* and crowned by the usual finial denoting the highest Buddhist heaven. Often the superimposed *chhatras* are decorated with small metal bells (Fig. 42).

If we compare the top storey of the Yākushiji temple with the tee of the Sārnāth *stūpa* (Fig. 21), it is clear that the latter is a stone model of a structure like the former. The curved eaves of the roof, the ends of the angle rafters, and the tall *chhatrāvali* decorated with nine *chhatras* are all faithfully reproduced in stone.

In Japan, the roofs are usually covered with tiles, but sometimes small copper plates like those still used in Malabar protect the roofs of the more important shrines.

The remarkable similarity between the wooden temples of India and those of China and Japan, clearly denotes a common origin for both styles of architecture. Since there is no evidence that buildings in this style existed in China or Japan prior to the sixth century A.D., while there is ample proof that they were common in India long before that date, there is no possibility of the Indian temples having been derived from Far Eastern prototypes.

Fig. 1

MODERN CEREMONIAL UMBRELLA, MADRAS.

Fig. 2.

MODERN CEREMONIAL UMBRELLA, MADRAS (DOMED TYPE).

Fig. 3.

THE BUDDHA'S DEATH, GANDHĀRA SCHOOL (CIRCA 200 A.D.).

Fig. 4.

THE BUDDHA'S FUNERAL-CAR, GANDHĀRA SCHOOL.

Fig. 3.

KŌTA FUNERAL-CAR, NILGIRIS, INDIA.

Fig. 6.

HINDU FESTIVAL-CAR, MADRAS.

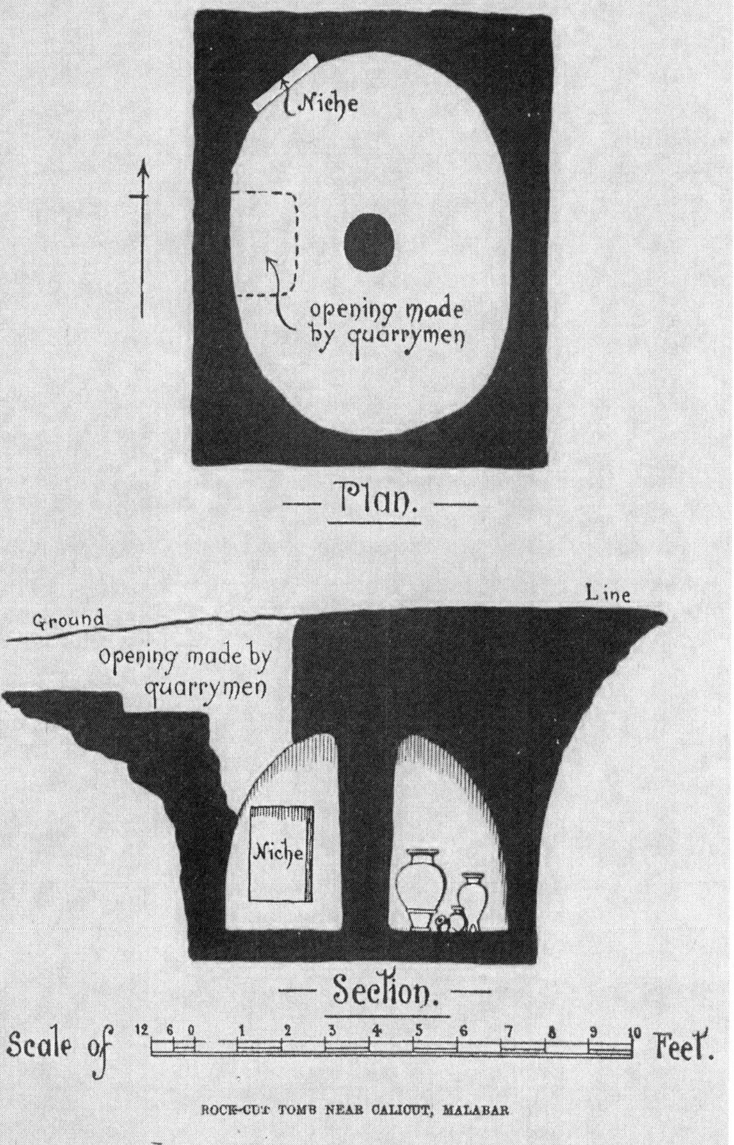

ROCK-CUT TOMB NEAR CALICUT, MALABAR

Fig. 8.

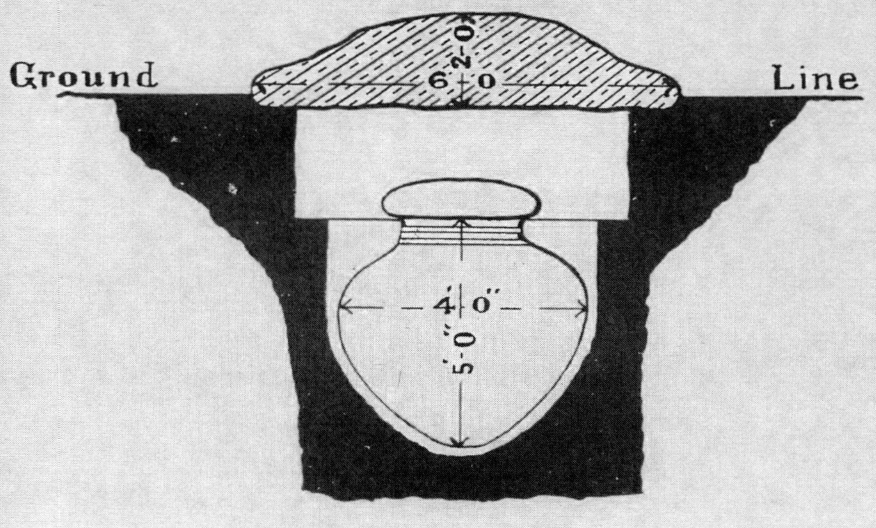

KODA-KALLU TOMB, MALABAR.

Fig. 9.

ŌDA-KALLU MEMORIAL, MALABAR.

Fig. 10.

STONE MEMORIAL UMBRELLA, MYSORE.

Fig. 11.

CHAMBERED TUMULUS, MADRAS.

Fig. 12.

CHAMBERED TUMULUS, MADRAS, WITH COVERING SLAB PARTLY REMOVED.

Fig. 13.

TYPES OF EARTHENWARE VESSELS FOUND IN TUMULI, ROCK-CUT TOMBS AND BURIAL URNS IN SOUTHERN INDIA.

Fig. 14.

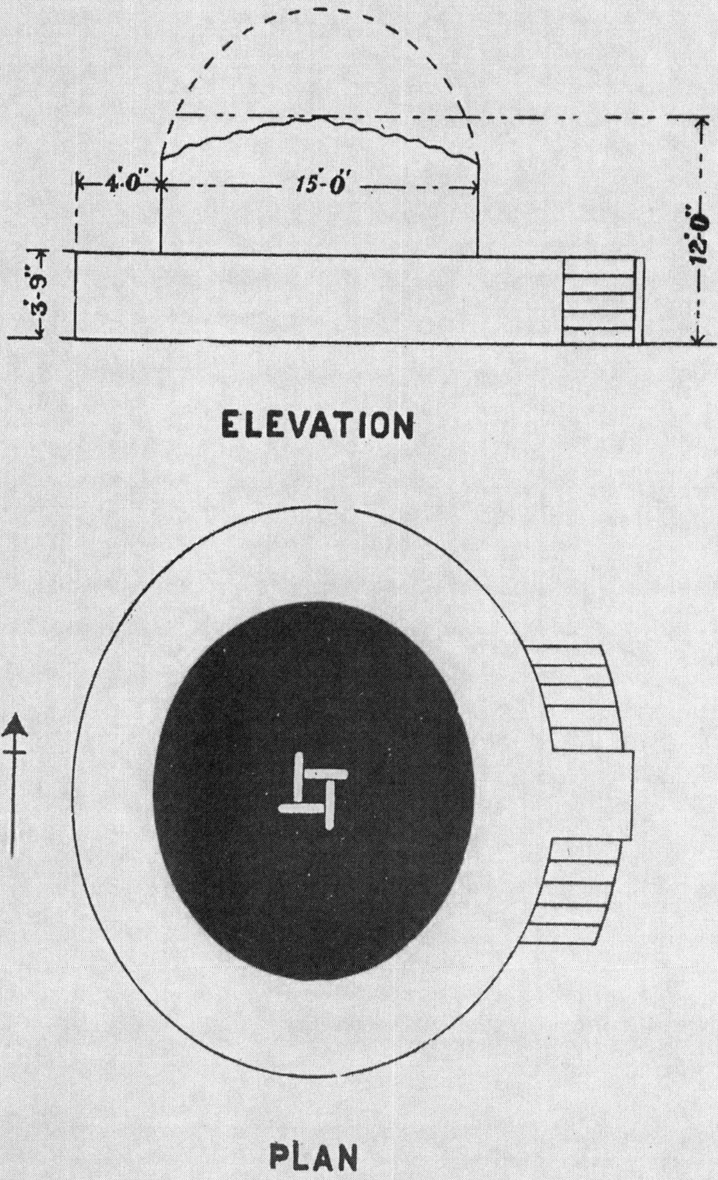

ANDĒR STŪPA, BHOPAL STATE (CIRCA 250 B.C.).

Fig. 15.

SANCHI BAS-RELIEF SHOWING EARLY TYPE OF STŪPA (COMMON ABOUT 200 B.C.).

Fig. 16. SANCHI STUPA, EAST VIEW.

Fig. 17.

SĀNCHĪ STŪPA, EAST GATEWAY.

Fig. 18.

ROCK-CUT STŪPA AT KANHERI, EARLY TYPE.

Fig. 19.

ROCK-CUT STUPA AT DHAMNAR, LATER TYPE.

Fig. 20

ROCK-CUT STŪPA AT AJANTA, LAST STAGE.

Fig. 21.

STONE MEMORIAL STŪPA FROM SARNĀTH NEAR BENARES, LAST STAGE.

Fig. 23.

SVAYAMBHŪNĀTH STŪPA, KĀTHMANDŪ, NEPĀL.

Fig. 23. SAPADA STUPA, PAGAN, BURMA, EARLY TYPE.

Fig. 24.

TAWYAGYAUNG STUPA, MANDALAY, LAST STAGE.

Fig. 25.

EARLY BUDDHIST TEMPLE AT NYAUNGU, BURMA

Fig. 26.

LATER BUDDHIST TEMPLE AT PAGĀN, BURMA.

Fig. 27. LATE BUDDHIST TEMPLE AT NALANDA, BIHAR.

Fig. 28.

DRAVIDIAN HINDU TEMPLE, MADRAS.

Fig. 29

COLOSSAL JAIN STATUE OF GOMATA RĀYA, KĀRKALA, SOUTH KANARA.

Fig. 30.

STONE DHŪPE AT MŪDABIDIRI, SOUTH KANARA.

Fig. 31.

BRASS MODEL OF THE JAINA HEAVEN, SOUTH KANARA.

Fig. 32.

WATER PAVILION, KRISHNA TEMPLE, UDIPI, KANARA.

Fig. 33.

EAST ELEVATION OF THE MAHADEVA TEMPLE, BEYPORE, MALABAR.

Fig. 31.

ENTRANCE TO THE BEYPORE TEMPLE, MALABAR.

Fig. 35.

EAVES OF THE BEYPORE TEMPLE, MALABAR.

Fig. 36.

HIMALAYAN RATHA, SARĀJ.

Fig. 31.

UMBRELLA ROOF OF AN OLD SIVA TEMPLE AT KUMHĀRSEN, SIMLA DISTRICT.

Fig. 38.

ANCIENT WOODEN TEMPLE AT DALAS, KULU.

Fig. 39.

TEMPLE OF TRIYUGA NARAYANA AT DYĀR, KULŪ.

Fig. 40.

HIDIMBĀ TEMPLE AT MANĀLI, KULŪ.

Fig. 41.

TEMPLE OF BHAIRAB, PATAN, NEPĀL.

Fig. 42.